MW01107635

# POINTS ON MADNESS

*Essays on Abnormal Psychology*

*David Liebert*

POINTS ON MADNESS:
ESSAYS ON ABNORMAL PSYCHOLOGY
© 2017 David Liebert

Cover photography by Misha Sokolnikov.

ISBN-13: 978-1546468776

Open Knowledge Books
http://www.openknowledgebooks.com

Author royalties have been assigned to Feeding Tampa Bay. Learn more about the work of this charity at feedingtampabay.org

*I can calculate the motion of heavenly bodies but not the madness of people.*

*-Isaac Newton*

# Contents

# 1 Introduction

Archeological findings dating back to 6,500 BC suggest the first attempt to offer care for those suffering from madness took the form of *trepanning* where the disturbed where held down while a jagged hole was cut through the skull revealing the brain. The belief is this earliest form of psychosurgery was done in an effort to allow evil spirits to escape in an attempt to return the patient back to a state of sanity (Nolen-Hoeksema, 2014). Examination of these primitive skulls reveals the presence of new bone tissue, evidence many of these patients survived their treatment. Moreover, the presence of multiple trepanned holes demonstrating various degrees of new bone growth suggests some patients underwent the procedure more than once.

The belief madness is the result of evil spirits lodged within the skull is just one early idea attempting to explain the causes for what a given society deems to be madness (what most textbooks would describe using terms such as *abnormal psychology, mental illness* or *psychopathology*.) Other ideas have gone on to suggest madness resulted from an improper balance of bodily fluids requiring the patient be bled. This was a treatment first prescribed by the ancient Greek physician Hippocrates (460–370 BC) and continued to be practiced by Benjamin Rush (1746-1813) who was the first American psychiatrist and established the first department of psychiatry at the University of Pennsylvania. Other ideas assumed madness to be an act of witchcraft requiring the patient be burnt alive (Szasz, 1970). Today, some might argue madness is best explained as a criminal behavior seeing

· Trepanning
· Benjamin Rush (1746) First American psychiatrist.

that roughly 64% of prison inmates have a diagnosable mental illness (Steadman, Osher, Robbins et al., 2009).

While some looked to the gods and others directed focus to the coursing blood through the body in an attempt to understand the nature of madness, it was the French psychiatrist, Philippe Pinel (1745-1826) who first adopted the practice of documenting the various symptoms and behaviors witnessed in his patients. He began to organize his observations, directing his attention to the symptoms as the source for gaining an understanding as to the true nature of madness. His efforts resulted in one of the first classification systems for operationalizing normal from abnormal behavior, earning him the title as "the father of modern psychiatry." Pinel's classification of madness (perhaps, now more appropriately operationalized as "mental illness") was based on a new idea. At root was emotional corruption (what he referred to as "moral") and could only be treated through a "moral therapy" grounded in emotional support and personal encouragement (Porter, 2002).

Pinel's efforts allowed the practice of mental health to transition from one oriented on *madness* to one now oriented on *mental illness*. This new orientation was now based on vetting behavior against a defined classification system, thereby, providing direction and order to operationalizing such phenomenon. Mental illness transitioned into an objective phenomenon and could now be empirically investigated, unlike madness where empirical techniques can't capture such subjective states of frenzied mayhem. Based on this foundation offered by Pinel, modern psychiatry would continue to organize itself around the classification of mental disease categories as modeled initially by Pinel.

This approach to empirically validate psychiatric states of mental illness through the use of categorization

· phillippe pinel 1745

was, once again, validated in 1952 when the American Psychiatric Association published the first edition of the *Diagnostic and Statistical Manual of Mental Disorders* (DSM). At first the document, not much larger than a pamphlet, was essentially ignored by the profession. Nevertheless, over the years it underwent several revisions: DSM-II (1968), DSM-III (1980), DSM-IIIR (1987), DSM-IV (1994), DSM-IV-TR (2000) and the DSM-5 (2013). Since the time of the first edition, the DSM has become the standard classification system for making a clinical diagnosis. All mental health professions (i.e., psychiatrists, clinical psychologists, mental health counselors, marriage/family therapists) are trained in using this diagnostic classification system. The 947 page document includes more than 300 specific mental health diagnoses.

The idea to question the empiricism of mental illness now filtered through more than a half century using the DSM might appear as outrageous as calling into question Isaac Newton's assumptions supporting notions on gravity. Nonetheless, the intent of *Points on Madness: Essays on Abnormal Psychology* is to distract the reader away from this objective study of abnormal psychology by embracing the subjective elements of this topic, and by doing so, brace for the pandemonium that may follow. Each essay is discrete but loosely organized around three themes; still, each essay asks the reader to consider some aspect of madness unanchored from the empiricism typically insulating the topic of mental illness.

The first five essays address the subjective nature of psychological theory. In these essays, several arguments are asserted. For instance, the role of the practicing psychotherapist is best carried out when approaching his or her patient from the point of view of *artist* than that of *scientist*. The effective psychotherapist is one who merely practices

· 1952 First DSM

the art of psychotherapy which is only informed by its science. Looking at mental illness strictly from an objective reality denies the fact that—with few exceptions—there is no empirical evidence to substantiate that mental illness even exists. We don't find use of objective measures such as blood tests, CAT scans, genetic screening or X-Rays used in the diagnosis of a mental illness because mental illness can't be seen in either bone, blood or flesh. Moreover, ignoring the subjective side to mental illness has merely resulted in a proliferation of new diagnoses in more recent years.

The latter chapters shift focus away from theory towards the practice of psychotherapy. There are times where patient-goals and the role the psychotherapist asserts to help the patient achieve their goals are from a distance as absurd as any of Albert Camus' stories. Yet, society's stigma of the mentally ill is as real as a snakebite. Finally, the subjective influences cradling psychology as empirical science are approached by acknowledging times where clinical practices are changed or prescribed, not because of science but due to decisions made by the courts or by writers of fiction or the actors portraying the mentally ill when a novel is brought to the silver screen.

*Points on Madness: Essays on Abnormal Psychology* is more a book of riddles then a textbook where the answers are to be found. These riddles remind me of a similar one posed to Alice by the Mad Hatter when he asks Alice, "Why is a raven like a writing desk? ...Have you guessed the riddle yet?" "No, I give up," Alice Replies. The Mad Hatter answers, "I haven't the slightest idea" (Carroll, 1984, p. 56).

# 2 Riddles in Art, Science and Psychotherapy

I began my college career back in the late 1980s initially as a history major. I remember taking an introduction to sociology class because it could be used to satisfy a graduation requirement that couldn't otherwise be satisfied in the history department. It was a chapter on social psychology that proved to be my downfall as a history major. I remember my professor rushing through the classroom door exactly one minute after the start of class, as she always did, ranting. That was her style: hit the door teaching! "I'll give you $20 to kill someone for me. $20! $20! Not a quick death, perhaps a painful death, but a good death!" She started pointing to some of us, "What about you John?" She waved a Jackson at John. She flapped the twenty at me. All I could do was give my head a simple shake no. My professor was a little "touched" as a few of them were who survived the 1960s. I remember appreciating her classroom dramatics, but the idea of committing a murder simply to pocket a $20 seemed a foolish question from the start. Of course no one seriously would entertain the idea of mortally harming another human being for profit, at least not for such a megger sum.

"Yes you would David. For a $20 I'll make a killer out of you!" We were then introduced to Stanley Milgram who had done just that very thing for merely $4.50. The study was conducted in the psychology laboratory at Yale University back in the early 1960s. Subjects were given a stipend of $4.50 to participate in a study looking at the effects punishment would have on learning. At least that was what the subject was told. Actually, Milgram was looking to see if the subject would be willing to deliver increasingly harmful electrical shocks to a fellow subject who was a confederate serving as an actor for Milgram. The confederate screamed in painful agony to the shocks being administered anxiously by the actual subject while another actor wearing a white lab coat rambled on as part of the script, "The study requires that you continue. There will be no permanent tissue damage." Amazingly, two-thirds of the time, the subject would follow the requests of the experimenter and deliver (at least what the subject believed to be) harmful electrical shocks to a lethal degree.

I was always amazed how those 50 minutes of class-time collapsed into what felt to me to be just a few minutes at most. Right at the 50 minute mark my professor again reached into her pocket taking out the 20-dollar bill, slapped it down on the desk at the front of the room she sometimes sat on top of during class and yelled, "Damn it! Yes, you would! Hell, I would've!" She stormed out of the classroom leaving us all in the packed classroom on the verge of PTSD. It was at that moment I was bitten. My professor was right. If I had been seated behind Milgram's shock-box, taunted by the experimenter to continue, deep down in my craw, I know I would have hit that button too. I understood this to be true, as true as I first believed just 50 minutes before that I would never do such a thing. How can this juxtaposition that exists between how we believe we will behave be rectified with the realities of our actual behavior? Although the paperwork followed at the end of the semester, I changed my major at that moment, just twenty feet away from an unsecured twenty-dollar bill.

I have now been teaching psychology for nearly two decades. This discipline sustains me. I love it because it is a series of unsolved riddles. You can spend a career tinkering with these riddles of human complexity, never coming to any final resolution. I think for this reason I would hate being a math teacher where the answers are clear and univocal. The answers to questions are never as much fun as the questions themselves. I say that "I love" the study of psychology, but I don't "love" psychology in a Romeo and Juliet sort of way. I "love" psychology more in the way some folks love horror movies. There is something about psychology that torments me in the sense that beauty torments the artist or words do the poet. It's the riddles of psychology that keep me captivated, and—by far—the biggest riddle I have encountered yet in psychology is that of mental illness. What is it? For me there is no greater mystery in psychology. In the classroom, from a far, buried in the textbook, I'm easily convinced no such phenomenon exists. Mental illness is as factual as unicorns and leprechauns; the phenomenon is nothing more than a fabrication fused together by social forces. Yet, in the time I've spent with patients as a psychotherapist, I can't imagine anything more real and true. Mental illness, from this perspective, is as real as teeth are for a dentist. I hope that I never find the answer to this question: what is mental illness? There would be little left in this field to sustain me then.

These words are personal, but so is the study of psychology for any student. The practice of psychology is not supposed to be a spectator sport. Moreover, I think it is essential for psychology students to embrace the ambiguity that exists in this field. Perhaps I'm mistaken; nevertheless, I teach my abnormal psychology class based on the premise that each-and-every one of my students are vetting the possibility they may want to be a psychotherapist helping to cure the depressed, psychotic and anxious amongst us. Here is my litmus test for such students: if one can be captured by psychology's ambiguity, they have identified the right field of study and, perhaps, even the right vocation. This is my primary objective for this collection of essays; it's an attempt to hook the interests of psychology students, getting them captured in the many folds and ravels of this riddle too. To this end, this book offers no answers, just questions.

There is another purpose for this book too. It's an opportunity for me to share a secret and—doing so—find some cathartic release for myself. Here's my confession: I don't believe the practice of psychotherapy is a science. Rather, the practice of psychotherapy is an art merely informed by science. I acknowledge there is something a bit blasphemous about this statement. This may be the case, in part, because psychotherapists place too much emphasis on the importance of science over other, less objective means of "knowing." After all, every introduction to psychology textbook starts the first chapter off by defining psychology as a science. *Psychology is a scientific study of behavior and mental activity*, that's what the textbooks all say. Moreover, every introduction to psychology textbook also includes a chapter on psychology's use of the scientific method, and how knowledge in the field is gained through the meticulous use of methodologies such as correlation and experimentation. Students are taught right from the start of their education in psychology that empirical science is the discipline's keystone. It would only make sense that any course in abnormal psychology should also define this subfield of as a "scientific study" too, but abnormal psychology is different from other subfields in psychology. Empirical science, in this case, shouldn't lead, rather it should follow. When empirical science takes the lead in abnormal psychology the waters get muddied. What appears to be clear and obvious only delivers us to the next ring of the onion. The concept of abnormal psychology, for instance, is one where the definition of the concept looms on the tongue, but still the speaker is unable to spit out the correct words. Although there is language to describe the phenomenon of mental illness, it always falls short and incomplete of the mark. This occurs because science is unable to empirically validate such definitions.

Science requires objectivity, where the researcher must assert his or her independence over the phenomenon being studied, even if that phenomenon is another person. There can be no bridge joining the two through emotions, social interests or personal values that might permit the transfer of corrupted observations thereby tainting the scientist's clarity, focus and—in so doing—findings. Such an approach, however, lacks any aesthetic quality; there is no opportunity for the evaluator to infuse his or her sense of balance between opposing observations of normal or abnormal. This notion of *balance* is what I am referring to as *art* when I suggest the practice of psychotherapy is an art informed by a science. This art, moreover, only comes into any sense of focus when subjective tools are employed. The psychotherapist who uses his or her subjective skills not only engages the imagination, but is now capable of projecting the emotions, social concerns and values of the patient onto him or herself. It is empathy that permits the psychotherapist to experience the other side of reality belonging to the patient. For the psychotherapist, cultivating his or her skills in empathy is more vital than developing those skills as a scientist. Again, art must proceed science in the clinical dynamic between psychotherapist and patient.

Empathy is the single essential tool for the psychotherapist. Establishing this empathetic connection to the patient is the act of psychotherapy. One might practice cognitive psychotherapy, existential psychotherapy or analytic psychotherapy, but the single characteristic running consistently through these various psychological denominations is the act of *psychotherapy*. Psychotherapy is a conscious, deliberate act of experiencing an exchange of empathy between the psychotherapist and patient with the attempt to be of some benefit to the patient. At those moments when the connection of empathy is established, the psychotherapist listens and the patient is understood and *psychache* ameliorates for the patient. Not only does it feel good to experience the empathy of another—simply put—it helps to improve that which hurts. Yet, this experience cannot be empirically measured. It is no more possible for a scientist to measure the ebb and flow of empathy being exchanged in the psychotherapist's office than it is to measure a mother's love for her child.

Great writers are also prolific readers. No artist creates without also consuming similar products produced by others practicing the trade. The same holds true for psychotherapists. The practice of psychotherapy as science has the student believe good psychotherapists have the diagnostic criteria memorized, easily decipher differential diagnoses in their head and apply an empirically validated treatment plan for the patient. Psychotherapy from this perspective is akin to a sort of mechanics. In this essay, rather, I've suggested the student consider the role of science as being secondary. Here science is only one factor used in the process of esthetic balance along with empathy. In this instance, psychotherapy is viewed as art. By adopting such a point of view, a warning needs to be heeded: the psychotherapist as artist is no different than the musician, poet or painter who attempts to touch the soul of humanity. One's now entered the ranks of those also tormented with an ideal.

# 3 Mental Illness as Snuffleupagus[1]

I began my graduate training back in the 1990s, first in sociology then in counseling psychology. I remember attending my first class in abnormal psychology, entitled *Psychopathology*. The Fourth Edition of the DSM was at that time the latest version of the American Psychiatric Association's "Psychiatric Bible" and served as our textbook for the class. The impressively large book was cloaked in a red cover, and I could not help but wonder if there just might be some connection between the color of the cover and Salinger's *Catcher in the Rye*. The syllabus had been reviewed, and the class was about one hour into a one-way discussion on the organization of the DSM into various categories of abnormal behavior and how such abnormality was assessed and determined per the five-axis model. The professor paused, made eye contact with the class, and asked if there were any

---

[1] Like most young children in the 1970s, I spent many hours watching *Sesame Street*. Big Bird's best friend was Snuffleupagus, an imaginary character only he could see. The other characters on the show would tease Big Bird when he spoke of his friend, as the woolly mammoth-like animal would have just wandered off the scene as others happened to have just walked on to the scene. No one would ever believe Big Bird's friend was real. I later learned at some point in the 1980s everything changed. Big Bird convinced the others Snuffleupagus was real by offering empirical evidence; he showed him to them. Now everyone knows the truth. Snuffleupagus is not imaginary; he is real, at least in a world where an eight-foot-tall yellow bird talks and has friends.

questions so far. I asked, what would turn out for that class to be my first and last question: "what's the difference between normal and abnormal behavior?" The professor looked for a moment to be stumped and then a spark of anger seemed to pulse through him as his eyes squinted. His reply was quick and sharp; "The behaviors found in the DSM are abnormal behaviors, and normal behavior refers to everything else not included in the DSM."

My professor's definition for *abnormal,* as it turns out, is as viable as any other definition. The National Alliance on Mental Illness (NAMI), for instance, claims *abnormal* refers to "a condition that impacts a person's thinking, feeling or mood and may affect his or her ability to relate to others and function on a daily basis. Each person will have different experiences, even people with the same diagnosis" (2015, n.p.). Thomas Insel, the Director for the National Institute of Mental Health suggests disorders labeled as *abnormal* "appear to be disorders of brain circuits" (2011, n.p.). The DSM-5 now offers a revised definition:

> A mental disorder is a syndrome characterized by clinically significant disturbance in an individual's cognition, emotion regulation, or behavior that reflects a dysfunction in the psychological, biological, or developmental processes underlying mental functioning. Mental disorders are usually associated with significant distress in social, occupational, or other important activities. An expectable or culturally approved response to a common stressor or loss, such as the death of a loved one, is not a mental disorder. Socially deviant behavior (e.g., political, religious, or sexual) and conflicts that are primarily between the individual and society are not mental disorders unless the deviance or conflict results from a dysfunction in the individual, as described above. (American Psychiatric Association, 2013, p. 20)

Thus, leading authorities in the field suggest the experience of a psychologically *abnormal* state may be rooted in the psychological, or maybe not. *Abnormal* "appears" to be neurological, as if to suggest that appearances might be deceiving at first glance. It is not *abnormal* for an individual to rant at their local government official unless such ranting is because one is, in fact, *abnormal*. Again, my professor's attempt to define *abnormal* by identifying just those conditions recognized in the DSM was as concise as other definitions.

Attempts to lock down and define what is, in fact, *abnormal* seem to fall short. Graduate and undergraduate courses entitled Abnormal Psychology, alike, quickly gloss over definitions, rushing to get to the actual disorders themselves (i.e., schizophrenia, posttraumatic stress disorder or disruptive mood dysregulation disorder), where definitions appear to be more concise. By doing so, however, students are left with the false impression a clean seam exists between what we know for certain about the true meaning of *abnormal* and what is unknown about its true nature when, in fact, there is a substantial gap between these two points of the known and the unknown. Since the 1990s, the DSM has gone through two revisions. The Fifth Edition (2013) contains 947 pages packed full of specific psychological disorders; yet, despite the clearly spelled out criteria necessary to diagnose each one of these abnormal conditions, there is still no single, clear thread weaving through all the DSM shedding light on what *abnormal* means.

Several factors help to create this illusion of a clean seam, rather than an actual gap, between specific diagnoses of abnormality outlined in the DSM and a basic, fundamental definition for what is, in fact, *abnormal*. First, we believe the meaning for *abnormal* is clear and essentially univocal because it is explained by experts in the fields of psychology and psychiatry. The scientific revolution has shown how wrong and backward our assumptions had once been regarding many wildly held beliefs (i.e., the earth is flat and at the center of the universe). Historical bias has primed us to see similar naivety in understanding the abnormal in terms of demonic possession, witchcraft or astrological influences as was the case in past centuries. We falsely assume if psychologists and psychiatrists endeavor to treat and care for the abnormal, they must have a clear idea of its true nature; yet, such an assumption is akin to a lawyer understanding the true nature of justice because she appears daily in a courtroom or an artist knowing the real meaning of beauty because he can paint a flawless portrait.

Second, the equivocal meaning for abnormal is wrongly blamed on the equally equivocal approaches to which mental health professionals are trained. Psychiatrists complete medical school earning an M.D. degree before embarking on a psychiatric residency. Their training involves heavy exposure to biology and pharmacology. Whereas, the clinical psychologist completes graduate school earning a Ph.D. or Psy.D. degree. Unlike the psychiatrist, the clinical psychologist cultivates expertise in psychometric testing and highly developed modalities of talk therapies. Yet, it is incorrect to assume the psychiatrist and clinical psychologist are looking at differing attributes of the same phenomenon biased by their respective training. This is not the same as two persons looking at a single orange where one sees only the juice to be yielded from the fruit while the other does not see past the rind for the prospect of making marmalade.

Third, the true meaning of abnormal is not revealed through the successful treatment of it. The last twenty years of psychology has witnessed a proliferation of empirical research attempting to identify the most effective treatments

for specific disorders. For instance, current research findings suggest psychopharmacology is the most effective way
for treating schizophrenia and bipolar disorders, but not as
effective in the treatment for dysthymic depression where
cognitive behavioral therapy leads in outcome effectiveness.
Deductively, logic holds that if changing how we think
about things leads to feeling less depressed, the depression
must have been the result of faulty thinking in the first place.
Moreover, if blocking the flow of dopamine in the brain results in unraveling the delusions and silencing the auditory
hallucinations, schizophrenia must be the result of too
much dopamine in the brain. The etiology (or cause) of an
abnormal condition and prescribing the best treatment for
the condition are discrete phenomenon. The two are not
necessarily casually linked. If aspirin may ameliorate one's
headache, it does not prove the headache was first caused
by having a lack of aspirin in the body.

  Finally, identifying the etiology of one disorder
does not extend to all disorders found in the DSM. For instance, those who are proponents of the medical model, believing the etiology for all forms of abnormality are brain-
based, oftentimes cite schizophrenia to support their claim.
Although, no "schizophrenic gene" has yet to be identified,
there is sound, logical evidence to suggest there just might
be such a gene to be found. For instance, the general population is at risk for this specific type of abnormality at the
rate of near 1%, but if the same person who is a sibling to a
monozygotic (identical) twin who has already been diagnosed with schizophrenia, the rate of risk will rise to near
48%, suggesting a strong biological influence. Nevertheless,
even if such a schizophrenic gene were to be identified, it
does not mean that all the other disorders in the DSM must
share a similar etiology too. Understanding the etiology of

etiology-cause

abnormal conditions must be addressed discretely from one disorder to the next.

Yet, despite the inherent limitations for suggesting a concise and certain meaning for the word, abnormal, the profession of psychology carries on with confidence that abnormality is real and true. Perhaps, there is a fundamental need to sort and organize the entire lot of humanity in categories of normal and abnormal. Such an appreciation appears to be inherent in us. We teach small children not to point and stare at disfigurements and oddities they notice in others. We reprimand children when they tease or bully other children due to believed weaknesses. At play, we see preschoolers automatically seek out those of the same sex to play with. Teenagers worry endlessly if their dress, hairstyle, playlists will be adversely judged by their peers. There is more to this phenomenon than just merely wanting to fit in; we need to connect to others. We need to be normal.

Unlike other species whose survival relies primarily on instincts, humans have developed a highly evolved process of *social cuing* to protect against those forces that may jeopardize survival. We look to the behavior of others to suggest how we ought to behave. When the fire alarm goes off in the movie theater, for instance, most people first look around to see if others are getting up to leave. Therefore, being an abnormal person may compromise one's ability to effectively rely on social cuing and, in turn, increase potential harm coming to one's self. Additionally, we want to make sense out of our world. In the face of unexplainable human events, applying the label of abnormal may help the event make sense, and, in so doing, promote a stronger sense of cohesiveness within the group. As Rudyard Kipling reminds us:

> All good people agree,
> And all good people say,

All nice people, like Us, are We
And everyone else is They

Finally, our instinct for survival demands we strive to be well. Facing the realization that one is abnormal, the logical reaction is to ameliorate the situation, turn the tide, and seek to be normal.

Identifying normal from the abnormal is not difficult at all when a physician identifies a patient's body temperature to be 102 degrees. Such a temperature for a person is abnormal. We know this to be certain because such a temperature cannot be sustained indefinitely; the individual will surely die. Should one look out the window and see a person flying in the sky wearing a red cape; that too would be abnormal. People do not have the ability to fly—no one ever has, and no one ever will. The challenge, however, for defining a person as abnormal based on thoughts, feelings and expressions of personality is that these are metaphysically grounded in the abstract, rather than the empirical. On what basis, can it be determined to be normal to cry at a funeral but abnormal for someone else to laugh at the same funeral? Psychologists are tasked with the impossible challenge of operationalizing a concept that only exists within the context of a human being's consciousness but still must do so within the context of the world human beings inhabit, suggesting the term abnormal to be used when states of psychological functioning are suspicious and are being called into question.

It is not surprising that many psychology textbooks on abnormal psychology quickly rush the process of defining the term, moving right on to lengthy discussions pertaining to specific mental illness, while altogether ignoring any definition on the term *normal,* for it is easier to identify what might not be normal than what is actually normal. Moreover, what attempts that have been made to define what is abnormal move so rapidly through the discussion leaving little opportunity to take note on any illogical assumptions upon which the definition rests. Most textbooks rely on four possible definitions to identify the presence of psychological functioning that appears to be abnormal.

In some instances abnormal is determined when the phenomenon is deemed to be *statistically rare.* Behaviors occurring infrequently in the human population are identified as abnormal simply because the needle has been found in the haystack. For instance, most the population (about 67%) has an Intelligence Quotient (IQ) ranging between 85 and 115, and about 95% of the population has an IQ score ranging between 70-130. When a psychologist identifies an IQ of 55, a diagnostic label must be provided to explain the unusual score, since an IQ of 55 is considered abnormal. It might be that the individual has a developmental disorder, like Down's syndrome, or has Alzheimer's disease. The fallacy with relying on the notion of statistical rarity to determine what is abnormal from the normal is two-fold. First, there is a lack of uniformity applied to it. Although someone with an IQ of 145 might be referred to as *gifted*, the label of abnormal is not applied in this instance. Yet, an IQ of 145 is about as statistically rare as an IQ of 55. The use of statistical rarity serves as the basis for identifying abnormality some of the time, but not all the time. Second, the same cannot be said for defining normal. In other words, if that which is statistically rare defines what is abnormal, then normal should be defined as that which most conforms to the statistical norm. The most normal amongst us would be those that lack any variance, unique qualities, original abilities or fresh perspectives. From this point of view, the duller a person happens to be, the more normal the person is.

Other psychologists have adopted the approach of basing a definition of abnormal on the experience of *personal distress.* Should a feeling or behavior result in psychological angst, a label of abnormal ought to apply. There are multiple problems with such a definition. It assumes that which does not feel good must be explained as being abnormal. But, sometimes distress can be healthy. For instance, when experiencing states of anxiety, the nervous system readies the body by increasing our heart rate, diverting blood to more vital organs often leaving one with a feeling of being nauseous, and funneling our attention towards a perceived threat, but doing so might just keep us alive during times of danger, or from falling asleep when reading the book the night before the final exam. This idea fails to apply any sort of consistency to the phenomenon, rather, looks only to the effect. For instance, some students might truly jump for joy when learning a grade of B was earned in the class, while others might become seriously depressed upon learning the devastating news—a B was earned in the course. But, a B is a B is a B. A diagnosis of pancreatic cancer would never be applied so subjectively. Third, flipping the definition would suggest the absence of personal distress signifies being normal. Yet, there is nothing normal in feeling no distress whatsoever when a bear is charging at you.

Many definitions of abnormal involve social norms. Abnormal is identified in the face of *norm violation*. When one's behavior is expressed in a manner exceeding the boundaries of what a given society deems appropriate, one may be labeled abnormal. Again, the fallacies are multifaceted when applying a sociological perspective to abnormal. First, no culture is stagnated; all societies evolve and change, meaning that what is considered abnormal today might be redefined as normal at another point in time. For instance, homosexuality was once defined as mental illness but later removed as a psychiatric disease in need of treatment. Why cannot the cure for AIDS be as simple as removing it from

*stat r are*
*distress*
*norm vi olation*

the *International Classification of Diseases-10* (ICD-10)? This definition also can quickly absorb ideas of power and inequality. Those who have the power in any given society have the control over labeling those who are abnormal. Consider for example the exponential increase witnessed in the prevalence rates of children diagnosed with attention deficit hyperactivity disorder (ADHD). Some children advocates have suggested the real problem lies at the feet of parents who are too busy or indifferent to spend the necessary time with their children. When the child acts out in response, the parent quickly has the child labeled as abnormal, rather than the parenting style coming under scrutiny. Additionally, the other significant limitation of a definition involving norm violation is its lack of cultural diffusion. What is considered normal behavior for an American might be interpreted as a clear sign of mental illness in another part of the world. It would be like determining a temperature of 102 is abnormal to have in China but acceptable to experience in the United Kingdom. Confounding this definition, as well, is the blurring taking place along with other concepts such as morality, deviance and law. Norms, mores and folkways strike more towards an appreciation of a culture's value system then what is normal versus abnormal.

Finally, many psychologists speak to the notion of one's ability or inability to function as a means for defining what is normal or abnormal. When a mood or behavior *inhibits functioning* at a typical level, a label of abnormal might be applied. The primary fallacy here lies with the assumption that people need to always be functioning. *Idle hands are the devil's workshop* reflects the protestant work ethic preached from the pulpits early in our nation's history. The ethic has only exacerbated in modern years. Many adults report they would happily give up sex in exchange for an added hour of sleep. There are those times in our lives where absence of functioning is desirable, for example, grieving the death of a family member.

Again, the challenge for psychologists in defining a person as abnormal or normal subjectively based on thoughts, feelings and expressions of personality is that these are metaphysically grounded in the abstract, rather than the empirical. Psychologists are tasked with the impossible challenge of operationalizing a concept that only exists within the context of a human being but still must do so within the context of the physical world human beings inhabit. What exists, perhaps at most, as sparks of neurological static in the brain is being labeled in an empirical world where the emotions of our inner world tangle as human lives intersect. Any psychological model addressing what is to be considered normal versus abnormal can only be done so by abstractly taking this natural world and imposing a theoretical system of analysis around it. Any definition of abnormal can only work within a given theoretical system. Moreover, different theoretical systems express different sets of assumptions and consequences tethered to each theory as it concerns etiology, individual freedom, personal responsibility, inherent biological endowments and the ability to move from a state of abnormal back to normal. To gain any meaningful insight on what abnormal means within the broader field of psychology, it is necessary to tease out the presumptions made by different theories. The range by which different presumptions exist in relationship to each other begins to operationalize a more concise definition of abnormal, although be it rather extensive. By no means does this process clarify a rigidly narrow definition of what abnormal means. This process may not offer a bullseye but, rather points the archer in the general direction of the target.

# 4  Primordial Soup Tastes like Psychological Theory

Applying the label of normal or abnormal to a person's observed behaviors and presumed thoughts and feelings is no simple task. Psychologists do not have at their disposal objective assessment techniques to confirm the presence of abnormality in people, meaning, there are no blood tests, CAT scans, fMRIs, and/or genetic tests available to substantiate a person as, in fact, abnormal. Suppose, for example, a person enters a hospital's emergency room complaining of severe pain in their right leg. The emergency room physician orders an x-ray of the leg showing an obvious bone fracture in two separate locations of the leg. Here the diagnostic test reveals the presence of an actual ailment, a broken leg. Perhaps the patient, as well as the physician, both suspected the leg was broken to begin with. Nevertheless, until the x-ray confirmed the broken leg, the suspicion was merely an idea or theory. Pathologies the likes of cancer, diabetes and broken bones are based in objective reality. They do, in fact, exist and testing procedures that can confirm the existence of such a reality is referred to as an *objective test*.

Since nearly all mental illnesses are not yet empirically confirmed to exist, ideas about them are still just theories. Therefore, the assessment instruments psychologists rely on to inform his or her observations on psychopathologies are merely subjective in nature. For example, suppose a person enters a hospital's emergency room complaining of severe depression. The on-call psychiatrist is called in to assess the patient and administers a Beck Depression Inventory (BDI) assessment. The BDI consists of 21 multiple-choice questions. These questions attempt to quantify various symptoms such as sex drive, weight loss and fatigue. Based on a tallied score of 50, the psychiatrist determines the patient to be *severely* depressed. Unlike the x-ray, however, all the BDI is confirming is an idea agreed upon by mental health professionals that a score of 50 is severe; whereas, a score of 25 is only *moderate*. Moreover, such ideas are subjectively influenced by culture, as well as possible biases of the assessor. This is the flaw for relying on the BDI to determine the presence of depression, regardless if the said disorder is moderate or severe; there is an absence of context, since subjective data tends to ignore context. How important is it to know the age, sex or religious faith of the patient with the possible leg fracture? Would such information change the status of the leg? Now suppose the psychiatrist learns that the patient's pet cat died a week ago, keeping in mind that our culture underappreciates the love and intimacy fostered in relationships forged with pets? Absent context the lines between depression and sadness or tension and anxiety evaporate.

A mental illness can only exist and be completely understood when it is insulated inside a psychological theory. From such a perspective, mental illness becomes rational directing our thinking towards an understandable set of principles. Now, mental illness can be fully understood when it is juxtaposed to a set of assumptions that navigate how the world works. Since the establishment of psychology in 1879 by Wilhelm Wundt at the University of Leipzig, many theories have developed attempting to explain a complete explanation for the etiology of mental illness.

Sigmund Freud suggested in his 1900 publication, *The Interpretation of Dreams*, mental illness was the result of unconscious conflict. The psyche's ego buries unconscious conflict into the unconscious mind resulting in *neurosis* as ego energy is now being redirected towards unhealthy ends. Neurosis may play out in obsessions, depression, narcissism, etc. Regardless, such neurosis is functional since it prevents the unconscious material from becoming conscious which would result in *psychosis,* referring to a complete and absolute break with reality. Under this theoretical model, the goal of the psychotherapist is to identify the latent meaning of the unconscious material and safely encourage it to become conscious for the patient, thereby, freeing up healthy ego energy. Sigmund Freud proposed his creative idea in an era where the assumption had been to view the etiology of mental illness as organic. The biological theory assumes mental illness is a product of bone, blood or flesh. Today, ideas support disorders—such as depression—result from chemical imbalances in the brain. Mental illness is understood as something erupting in the synapse as the ebb and flow of neurotransmitters like serotonin and norepinephrine fail to launch from the synaptic vesicles in adequate supply. Their flow needs to be supported by chemical enhancements like Zoloft or Cymbalta.

It was in the 1920s when behavioral psychologist John B. Watson challenged the Freudian assumption which had become the dominant force in psychology by that decade. Along with his colleague, Rosalie Rayner, Watson demonstrated how a phobia might be better understood when viewing its' etiology from the perspective of behaviorism. By pairing an adverse stimulus to a white rat, a small child began to associate the two paired stimuli. Then when only the rat was presented, the child responded in phobic anguish. Watson and Rayner were able to demonstrate how the child's phobia of a white rat was learned rather than a result of a repressed defense mechanism. Its etiology was not the result of a failure within the system, rather an adverse environmental association. Other psychological theorists also challenged the assumption that human beings are passive and easily influenced by the world around them. Humanistic psychology assumes, for instance, human beings possess a strong internal force directing them to achieve internal potential. This may not occur, however, because of social problems inherent in the society.

Although all such theories offer context making mental illness understandable, such theories no not prove the existence of mental illness. Psychological theories are only capable of making assumptions and generalizations supporting a postulation that is embedded in a specific social context. For instance, theories on abnormal psychology make assumptions where the "problem" resides, suggesting the problem might be logged somehow in the person or in the environment. Theories also assume a degree of permeability exists with the problem as pathology flows between the person and his or her environment. For the discussion that follows, those theoretical models used to explain abnormal psychological functioning will be vetted on a schema of an intersecting horizontal and vertical continuum of *self* versus *environmental* and *closed* versus *open*. The *self* refers to all that makes up the essence of a human being, including anatomy, physiology, soul and psyche. Whereas, the *environment* simply refers to the space that one lives out his or her life, including geography, climate and all that goes into comprising a culture. A *Closed* system refers to an understanding towards abnormality, contending there is little interchange between the *self* and the external *environment*. These systems suggest little permeability between the person and the environment in which he or she experiences life. Abnormality resides, for the most part, either within the person (*self*) on in their *environment*. Whereas, *open* systems assume liberal permeability exists between the *self* and his or her *environment*.

A dynamic, symbiotic exchange occurs between the personal and the social. Abnormality is not seen as a disease agent, rather as a general failure in navigating a seamless disambiguation between the environment and the person. The intersection of the horizontal and vertical continuums results in four quadrants: *closed-self, closed-environment, open-self,* and *open-environment.* Different theoretical assumptions attach to each of the four quadrants.

*Closed-self* theories approach an understanding of abnormality by downplaying any role of one's free will, viewing those who are abnormal as being "sick" and powerless to ameliorate their abnormality on their own. Abnormality results from a chink in the system, over extending available resources, or when disease invades one's internal system. Understanding abnormality requires a reductionist approach by breaking down psychological phenomenon into finite pieces (i.e., reinforcers, neurotransmitters and defense mechanisms). To this end, tools of the trade need to be used (i.e., psychopharmacology or dream interpretation). Moreover, treatments to overcome abnormality view the inflicted as being passive and needing to be compliant to his or her treatment. Early and contemporary theories in psychology tend to align tightly to this quadrant (i.e., brain-based theories and psychoanalysis).

Whereas, *open-self* systems still look to the individual to identify the location where the abnormality lies, but this orientation hails the inherent free will we all possess, seeing the inflicted as playing an active role in ameliorating their negative psychological state. Thus, reductionism is not required, for it is the individual that lies as the basis of the exchange. No individual's experience is deemed truer than another's experience. Ameliorating the problem often involves a confrontation with the *self, environment* or the social experience.

Thus, treatment often involves embracing the relics of culture finding meaning in art, literature, philosophy and relationships with others.

FIGURE 1: Four Quadrant Model

CLOSED SYSTEM

| Closed-Self | Closed-Environment |
|---|---|
| Assumptions: Sick, Lacking Free-will, Disease within the system | Assumptions: Social Problems, "Problems of Living," Exploitation |
| Treatment: Compliance | Treatment: Sociological |
| Examples: Psychodynamic & Biological | Example: Anti-Psychiatry |

SELF                    ENVIRONMENT

| Open-Self | Open-Environment |
|---|---|
| Assumptions: Suffer & Free Will | Assumptions: Free Will & Human Concerns |
| Treatment: Truth, Journey, Confrontation | Treatments: Return to Self & Sociological |
| Examples: Behaviorism & Existential | Example: Humanistic |

OPEN SYSTEM

Again, environmentally orientated systems see the etiology of abnormality as residing in the environment, not the individual. Such a system assumes a sociological orientation for appreciating how it is the individual becomes labeled as abnormal. *Closed-environment* models take the position: that which is abnormally infected is not the individual, rather it is the environment that is diseased. People's psychological dispositions may range, but nowhere within the range does there exist any such thing as mental illness. In the words of Thomas Szasz, the disease of mental illness is a "myth." Rather, what does exist are those in a society who are unwilling to coexist with thoughts and behaviors that deviate from the established norm. Through the process of exploiting those who lack social status and power, the abnormal label is assigned to the individual. For instance, perhaps, the increased prevalence of American children misdiagnosed with attention deficit hyperactivity disorder (ADHD) has nothing to do with children who are inattentive and unable to sustain adequate focus and attention while in the classroom but has more to do with a school system increasingly relying on standardized testing to evaluate students'—as well as the school's—performance. Treatment for ADHD is simply for the benefit of the school's cumulative performance on standardized tests. Such ideas are expressed under the label of the anti-psychiatry movement.

Finally, *open-environment* models assume that abnormality resides in the environment but due to the porous boundary between the personal and the environmental, the individual has the ability and capacity to improve their psychological state by mentally overcoming environmental challenges. Humanistic theories, for example, reside in this quadrant. Consider Abraham Maslow who suggested our natural tendency was to grow towards *self-actualization*. "A musician must make music, an artist must paint, a poet must write, if he is to be ultimately happy. What a man *can* be, he *must* be" (Maslow, 2013, p. 23). If the aspiring painter never achieves her artistic potential, it is not because she lacks sufficient drive and determination. Rather, it is because society has presented her with barriers thwarting her development towards personal fulfillment. For instance, the college demands a prescribed curriculum including math, science and speech classes. On her third attempt at College Algebra, she finally gives up dropping out of college permanently. Why not—suggests Maslow—open the classroom up, allowing the aspiring young artist to now choose her own course of study, rather than prescribed courses. Better yet, why should her professors give her a syllabus outlining the learning objectives for the term, the young artist should present her professors with learning outcomes she wishes to achieve that semester?

This essay has attempted to explain the stance historically adopted by several dominant theories in abnormal psychology. The goal has been to show how these theories differ in orientation to perspectives on where the abnormal phenomenon resides—within the person or within the environment—and the degree of permeability existing between these two points. No theory has been championed over another. Moreover, many differences have been identified amongst the theories discussed. These differences have focused on the degree to which free will exists and the extent to which the patient has responsibility in both the etiology and treatment of the identified abnormal condition. Yet, despite these many differences, all these theories share a common factor: the abnormal condition emerges from a sort of primordial soup cloaked as psychology theory. For instance, abnormal *is* unconscious conflict as explained by the psychoanalyst. Abnormal *is* the result of environmental

associations according behaviorists or abnormal *is* a society's attempt to mislabel and exploit the weak amongst us,
so says the anti-psychiatrist.

To be an effective psychotherapist, one must enjoy
soup.

# 5 Ouch!

A frequent occupational challenge launched often at psychiatrists is that, unlike their colleagues practicing medicine in other areas of specialization, psychiatry isn't "real medicine," meaning psychiatrists don't actually practice medicine. After all, those making such critical commentary will point out that for most mental illnesses, there is no clear organic invasion of the body that can be identified as the etiology for the mental illness. The orthopedic surgeon pins a broken bone; the radiologist zaps cancer cells down to dust; the ophthalmologist removes the foggy lens restoring the patient back to 20/20 vision. Psychiatrists, however, merely have a pouch of pills in their medial arsenal targeting symptoms, not actual pathology.

In 1999 David Satcher, U.S. Surgeon General declared the first decade of the new century to be the *Decade of the Brain*; "we recognize that the brain is the integrator to thought, emotion, behavior, and health. Indeed, one of the foremost contributions of contemporary mental health research is the extent to which it has mended the destructive split between 'mental' and 'physical' health" (U.S. Department of Health and Human Services, 1999, preface). Since the publication of the U.S. Surgeon General's report on mental health, much attention in research along with tremendous sums of economic resources have followed all too empirically substantiate the biological basis for mental illness. Perhaps over concern that subjective analysis cannot yield and support objective theory, there seems to have been little research addressing a common complaint experienced by patients suffering from either biological illnesses (i.e., arthritis) or mental illnesses (i.e., generalized anxiety disorder): pain. Nevertheless, often what brings the patient into the psychotherapist's office is a desire to ameliorate their pain. Yet, most textbooks ignore this element as a possible attribute when defining the difference between psychological states of *normal* versus *abnormal*. Even the DSM-5 fails to reference the word "pain" in the book's index. In this essay, however, the goal is show that to experience a state of abnormal *means* to hurt, suffer and ache. Pain is as frequent a companion to mental illness as it is to physical, medical illnesses sharing many commonalities between these two categories of disorders. Yet, too quickly it may seem psychologists transition the definition for abnormal away from one that embraces ideas about *pain*, thereby, assuming psychological pain is somehow a related but discrete experience from that of physical pain. Moreover, in this instance the word *pain* becomes a sort of holophrase. It is a mistake to do so. Pain is pain regardless of its etiology. Like our initial attempt to define abnormal, there is also subjectivity associated with the definition of pain, but this subjectivity may be more similar than different when the concept of pain is being applied to organic disease.

One commonality between pain associated with both physical disease/injury and mental illness is its range of both presence and absence. Not all disease hurts. A physician assessing a patient for possible diabetes may ask questions pertaining to frequent urination, excessive thirst and dizziness, but the physician doesn't normally ask the patient about his or her severity of physical pain. The same holds true when evaluating for the presence of schizophrenia; here too, the patient isn't asked to report their level of pain. In addition, there are instances where it seems illogical for pain to be reported. For example, many people who experience the loss of a limb report pain, sometimes agonizing pain over the part of body now gone (i.e., phantom limb pain). There are also those instances where it makes no sense that pain is not being experienced (i.e., walking over hot coals while in a meditative state).

A second point of commonality between pain associated with physical disease/injury and mental illness is that both forms share similar makeups. An analysis of the various characteristics making up the phenomenon of pain speak towards both the physical/organic as well as the psychological/inorganic. To this end, attempts to define the nature of pain tend to involve the interaction of three confounding attributes. First, pain involves our senses. The transduction of pain is—in part—based on what we touch, see, smell and hear. The odor of decaying, rotting food may swiftly result in gaging and vomiting just as a piercing noise has us cupping our ears to deafen the sound. Our sensory systems (i.e., eyes and ears) are responsible for *transduction*, meaning the sensory organs (i.e., eyes) convert a raw stimulus (i.e., light wave) into a format interpretable to the nervous system. Second, pain involves emotion. Accompanied with pain is an internal, affective state. Psychological states of fear, anger, rage, alarm, disgust, dread and hate can all be felt at times of pain. The emotional expression witnessed for one who has just had a car door slam on their hand is indistinguishable from the anguish witnessed by another just learning the tragic news a loved one has died. Consider the pain disorder *asymbolia* where one is, in fact, physically sensitive to painful stimuli, but there is no emotional distress over the pain; one is capable of feeling pain without pain hurting the person. There is a sort of dissociation taking place much like when one experiences the benefits of morphine. Emotions are essential to the full experience of pain (Grahek, 2007). Finally, pain involves cognition. There must be an internal perceptual awareness of what is being experienced. *Perception* refers to the active meaning-making process that occurs as the sensation and emotion are interpreted. Perception is a cognitive process and significantly influences our personal experience of pain. Perception's role in the experience of pain helps to explain why pain awareness can change; although, there has been no change in the intensity of the pain stimulus. For instance, we have all had the experience of being distracted, perhaps in a conversation, losing immediate awareness of a headache or toothache that may have seemed intolerable just a moment prior. Additionally, numerous research studies have shown how catastrophizing anticipated pain does, in fact, heighten actual pain outcomes. Walking into the dentist's office anticipating pain will result in the actual experience of greater pain during the procedure.

The role perception plays in making emotional meaning may also help to explain why some sensations may be interpreted as painful for some but pleasurable to others. Consider, for example, *sexual masochism disorder* (SMD) which refers to a type of *paraphilia*, meaning one has an "intense and persistent sexual interest other than sexual interests in genital stimulation or preparatory fondling with phenotypically normal, physically mature, consenting human partners" (American Psychiatric Association, 2013, p. 685). In other words, a paraphilia refers to sexual arousal and/or sexual gratification by unusual means. With SMD, sexual arousal, pleasure, and gratification for the person is associated with experiencing humiliation, being beaten, and exposed to suffering. An essential component in making a diagnosis of SMD is "personal distress." Should one express no alarm, concern, or distress over this sexual interest, the diagnosis is not made, suggesting the sexual expression of masochism to be normal. Thus, some people (which the

American Psychiatric Association skeptically estimates to be less than 2% of the population) actually experience such pleasurable emotional states as euphoria, excitement, joy and love by being struck by the hand or other objects, having hot wax poured on the body or pinched with clamps.

Many experts in the field of pain study have attempted to classify and logically organize the phenomenon of pain. Some have done so based on pain's duration as either chronic, acute or transitory. Others attempts have organized pain around body locations (i.e., abdominal or cranial) or etiological factors like inflammation versus nerves. In the field of psychology, however, classification tends to organize pain as being either *psychogenic* or *algopsychalia* in nature. *Psychogenic pain* refers to an experience of pain resulting from psychological distress (Alexander, 2012). A student's anxious fear over tomorrow's classroom presentation results in a migraine, or he experiences gastrointestinal pain the week after his girlfriend left him for another man. The pain is not fictitious nor expressed as a ploy for attention. Suggesting an aspirin or antacid is as helpful of a remedy in such circumstances as if the headache resulted from excessive reading or heartburn following a spicy meal.

*Algopsychalia pain,* on the other hand, is experienced on the emotional level. It refers to a cognitive awareness of personal suffering, a mental pain with no expectation of linking it to a biological source (Blom, 2010). It is what suicidologist Edwin Shneidman has referred to as "psychache" (2002). There is a crisp recognition this pain comes, not from the nervous system, but from being human. The recognition may only exist at the emotional level absent the ability to articulate in language the feelings of loneliness, despair and estrangement that tend to often accompany it.

Perhaps, one of the most poignant descriptions of algopsy-chalia comes from journalist William Styron's personal memoir reflecting on his own battle with depression:

> What I had begun to discover is that, mysteriously and in ways that are totally remote from normal experience, the gray drizzle of horror induced by depression takes on the quality of physical pain. But it is not an immedi-ately identifiable pain, like that of a broken limb. It may be more accurate to say that despair owing to some evil trick played upon the sick brain by the inhabiting psyche, comes to resemble the diabolical discomfort of being imprisoned in a fiercely overheated room. And because no breeze stirs this caldron, because there is no escape from this smothering confinement, it is entirely natural that the victim begins to think ceaselessly of oblivion. (1990, p. 50)

Algopsychalia pain has been associated as being in-trapsychological, meaning the stimulus experienced is inor-ganic, occurring only within the mind, because there is not a clear and obvious sensory system involved in transduction. This assumption may be accurate or it may be mistaken. The idea humans have five senses (i.e., hearing, vision, taste, smell and touch) is wrong. Our senses also include: thermo-ception (temperature), mechanoreception (vibration), equilibrioception (balance), proprioception (kinesthetic), and chemoreception (internal chemical levels such as so-dium). There is still debate on the actual number of senses human beings are capable of possessing. Perhaps, algopsy-chalic pain results from the transduction of a stimulus ac-companied with an intense emotional perception resulting in a pain response.

A final commonalty between physical/organic pain and psychological/inorganic pain pertain the mutual benefits of psychotherapy. It would seem talking to a psycho-therapist about one's pain is helpful in curbing the experience of pain. Pertaining specifically physical/organic forms of pain, cognitive-behavioral therapy (CBT) has been shown to be helpful across a wide range of pain syndromes. Targeting a patient's beliefs and expectations about his or her pain helps the patient adjust to their experience with pain, report lower frequencies of painful episodes and report a reduction in their experience with pain intensity (Thomas, Wilson-Barnett & Goodhart, 1998). Thus, the experience of pain may also serve as a bridge for understanding the connections between organic and inorganic forms of disease.

# 6  Epidemiology[2] and the Manufacturing Mental Illness

If mental illness was a commodity traded on the stock-market, it would make for a fine investment, perhaps right up there with companies the likes of Apple or the Outback. The United States has witnessed an increasing incidence[3] trend with more Americans being diagnosed with a mental illness than in past decades. Per one recent national investigation on prevalence[4], approximately 9.8 million Americans have been diagnosed with a serious mental illness, making that about 4.0% of the U.S. population (Substance Abuse and Mental Health Services Administration, 2015). Moreover, another report suggests the extent of psychopharmacological use by Americans to be near 25% of the adult population (Jenkins, 2010). Since the first publication of the DSM in 1952, the manual documenting the sumtotal of mental illnesses has increased from 132 pages to 947 pages with the latest 2013 publication of the manual's fifth edition. The incidence rate for a range of mental illnesses has steadily increased over the years. As the number of clin-

---

[2] Epidemiology refers to the scientific study of patterns of health and illness within a given population.

[3] Incidence refers to the number of new cases of an illness diagnosed in a specific period.

[4] Prevalence refers to the proportion of a given population that has (or had) a specific diagnosis within a designated period.

ical psychologists along with other mental health professionals has increased[5] along with the soaring use of psychotropic medications in recent years, we have witnessed a
surge in the growth of mental illness. There is an obvious
positive correlation: as resources for treatment increase so
does mental illness' incidence, as if care and treatment serve
as a breading-ground for such pathology to erupt. Thus, the
real problem afoot may not be psychopathology—it self—
but the care and treatment for psychopathology. Such an
observation on its face would seem illogical: the care and
treatment of mental illness is possibly the cause for it.

   Some have suggested the statistical data to be mis-
leading, suggesting there has been no meaningful change in
incidence rates, especially with serious mental illness the
likes of psychosis. This is merely an instance where statistical analysis is chocking the data making it confess resulting
in a sort of false positive. Rather, the data is masked by the
ebb and flow of evolving social policies. For example, during the 1980s under the Regan Administration, community
mental health agencies engaged in the new policy of deinsti-
tutionalization resulting in the release of significant numbers of chronically mentally ill people from psychiatric facil-
ities onto the streets. This policy change reflected changes
in the ethical cannon suggesting involuntary treatment was
inappropriate for the chronically mentally ill, only voluntary
treatment was deemed ethical. Nevertheless, the era of de-
institutionalization resulted in a data shift where psychiatric
hospitalization decreased while the population in homeless-
ness surged.

---

[5] According to a recent report by the American Psychological
Association, there are currently 106,000 actively practicing clinical psychologists. Moreover, the number of psychologists enter-
ing the field has increased 3.2% from 2005 to 2013 (Lin, Nigrinis, Christidis & Stamm, 2015).

A rational, understandable sense for this data begins to emerge when a sociological lens is applied taking into an account various dynamic social factors. The discussion which follows suggests the increasing incidence of mental illness may be better understood in terms of sociological epidemiology then psychology or biological epidemiology. Social influences such as the media's glamorization of certain mental illness, social politics, society's attempt to ameliorate the stigma of mental illness and pedagogical changes in professional training for mental health providers explain this rising statistical trend.

Media Awareness

The DSM is not for casual reading. We do not find vacationers while on Spring Break lying out on Florida beaches leisurely skimming through DSM chapters on differential diagnoses such as that between anorexia nervosa with bulimia nervosa. Rather, most people—outside of professional circles—formulate their ideas about clinical psychology based on popular media: fictional books, television and movies, with this latter category, movies, being the most pervasive influence. "Films are especially important in influencing the public perception of mental illness because many people are relatively uninformed about the problems of people with mental disorders, and the media tends to be especially effective in shaping opinion in those situations in which strong opinions are not already held" (Wedding & Niemiec, 2014, p. 2). Movies have become an integral slice of our modern culture. In the last 16 years, total annual movie industry revenue has exceeded $10 billion. Americans love the movies. Movies can serve as a means by which we look at our culture from a far, question and advocate for social change. For example, the 1975 film *One Flew Over the Cuckoo's Nest,* based on Ken Kesey's novel of the same title, shook viewers to the core suggesting psychiatric hospitals are all harmful and demeaning institutions. Necessary or not, institutional reforms occurred in psychiatric hospitals because of this film.

Some have argued towards the film industry's general tendency to depict those suffering from a mental illness in negative terms, perpetuating stereotypes of the mentally ill as degenerates, dangerous and befuddled (Pirkis, Blood, Francis & McCallum, 2006). Yet, there is evidence to suggest the opposite: movies can encourage the public to feign psychopathology. The Paparazzi captures the image of Hollywood's newest star with her pocketbook slug over her arm casually strolling along Redo Drive, and the female population rushes to the malls to buy their version of the pocketbook before the shelves are left empty. People want to look like, dress like, eat like, vacation like and even suffer like their favorite movie star. The 1976 film *Sybil* demonstrates this point of *sine qua non*[6]. Sybil, played by Sally Field, is a young graduate student suffering from multiple personality disorder, what is now referred to in the DSM as dissociative identity disorder (DID). The disorder is characterized by having two or more distinct personality states and regular gaps in memory of daily events. As Wedding and Niemiec (2014) point out, prior to the movie's release, the psychiatric community considered DID to be an extremely rare condition with 80 individual cases in 1970 being reported. Following the movie's release in 1979, the incidence rate rose to 6,000 cases in 1986 and 40,000 cases by 1998. Today, the American Psychiatric Association estimates DID afflicts about 1.5% of the population. The steady exponential increase in incidence of DID begs the question to what extend

---

[6] Latin, referring to something that is essential and necessary to possess.

DID symptomology was influenced by movie watchers' desire to be just like Sally Field as well as those other actors who have portrayed this common psychopathology on the silver screen: *Raising Cain* (1992), *Primal Fear* (1996), *Fight Club* (1999), *Me, Myself & Irene* (2000), *Secrete Window* (2004), *Frankie & Alice* (2010), *Peacock* (2010) and *Split* (2017).

### The Social Politics of Power

Contributing to the trend maybe the process of ongoing revision of the DSM which seems to add new diagnoses with each revision. A closer look at this trend provides a basis to propose these new additions to the DSM are an attempt to address social concerns lying beyond the identified patient. The patient, in such instances is not of primary concern; the patient is merely serving to meet a broader social agenda. As the anti-psychiatry movement contends, the diagnosis of mental illness is a tool used by the socially powerful to squash the voice of the weak ensuring the status quo of power. As the mid-century and the politically radical decade of the 1960s unfolded, those entrenched in biologically minded approaches for defining the human condition tussled on with those from the Freudian side of the isle; new ideas explaining the human condition began commanding an audience. Academics and practitioners, alike, increasingly began to look outside of the individual to obtain a better appreciation for what human condition might be about, and it was beginning to be increasingly more porous and susceptible to the influences of the external world. From this vantage point, some began to propose that it is not the human organism that is vulnerable to those diseases-agents resulting in a flawed human state; rather, it is an infected or corrupt culture truly serving as the etiology for what has gone awry with the human. This being the case, for those who sought to blame an infected culture, they began to question the sincerity of the psychoanalytic model, along with all other psychological models, as a meaningful way to expressing the current state of human affairs. The practice of mental health by psychiatrists, psychoanalysts and clinical psychologists was coming under attack as a coercive, oppressive practice where the treatment was seen to be more dangerous to our psychological health.

Psychiatrist Thomas Szasz, following the publication of his *The Myth of Mental Illness* (1974) soon became identified as one of the leading proponents of this *anti-psychiatry* movement. In this book, Szasz argues that referring to mental illness in terms of a medical disease is simply mistaken since actual medical diseases are the result of a "lesion" of the body; there is something wrong with the body that can be empirically detected in either bone, blood, or flesh. Whereas, with mental illness there is nothing that can be identified as corrupt with the physiology and anatomy of the person. Rather, Szasz goes on to argue, what is referred to, as mental illness is better understood as merely "problems with living."

For those aligned with the anti-psychiatry movement, the fault lies in the culture and a profession willing to assign a label to those who do not conform to the expectations of the culture. As David Cooper, who coins the term "anti-psychiatry," explains, "I've been concerned with the question of violence in psychiatry and have concluded that perhaps the most striking form of violence in psychiatry is nothing less than the violence of psychiatry in so far as this discipline chooses to refract and condense on to its identified patients the subtle violence of the society it only too often represents to and against these patients" (1967, p. xii). In so doing, as sociologist Erving Goffman (1959) elaborates, the psychiatric patient does not experience any sort of real care or treatment. What the patient experiences is a "resocialization" where his or her true self becomes reoriented, polished down through a process of institutionalization. Here the patient comes to understand the real objective is to become "dull, harmless and inconspicuous" where, in turn, the true self is eroded away resulting in a chronic state of mental illness. Consider, just before reaching for the pillow at the end of the novel, Chief, the story's narrator from Kesey's *One Flew Over the Cuckoo's Nest* describes how R. P. McMurphy's eyes "stared into the full light of the moon, open and undreaming, glazed from being open so long without blinking until they were like smudged fuses in a fuse box" (1962, p. 275).

Critics of the anti-psychiatry movement are often quick to sweep such ideas under the rug, suggesting such folks are nothing more than religious zealots, leftist political radicals, or ivy tower idealists who have never actually been present with an anguished patient in the clinical consultation room. It would simply be hubris to witness psychological pain in another human being only to suggest its etiology is merely a "myth" cloaked in social fabrication. Nevertheless, it is an error to assume anti-psychiatrists do not acknowledge the realities of human suffering, and they are willing to forgo all concern for such suffering all to pursue radical political fights over the intellectual ownership of mental illness. Proponents of the anti-psychiatry movement are, in fact, concerned with addressing the needs of mental illness through patient-direct treatments. As Jacoby explains, "…there is no such activity as radical therapy—there is only therapy and radical politics… There is no shame in aiding the victims, the sick, the damaged, the down-and-out. If mental illness and treatments are class illness and treatment, there is much to be done within this realty" (1975, p. 139). Those who aligned themselves towards the anti-psychiatry movement, and worked professionally with patients, tend to cultivate approaches focused on acceptance, establishing friendships, and ensuring communication is being understood even if the patient was not expressing him or herself by using clear language. For instance, Scottish psychiatrist R. D. Laing established Kingsley Hall, a community care center in London that was free of restraint and use of antipsychotic medications. Clinical Psychologist David Smail (2005) built therapeutic alliances with his patients by focusing on the cultivation of friendships with his patients, believing that what everyone most needs are simply to be liked by others.

Anti-psychiatry advocates often see the assignment of the mental health label resulting from an imbalance of power. There is an exploitation of the powerful at the expense of the weak. In any psychotherapeutic relationship, the weakest amongst us are children whose consent for care, at best, lies in the hands of the parents or, at worst, lies in the hands of the state. The concern when labels of mental illness are assigned to children is that the assignment is done so to serve the interests of parents, foster-parents, teachers, and others at the expense of children. Mental health is thrusted upon the child simply for the purpose to restrain, increase academic performance, or demand social compliance.

A research study, partially funded by the National Institute of Mental Health, released in 2007, clearly stated there had been a 400% increase in the prevalence of children who had been diagnosed with a pediatric version of bipolar disorder in just a decade's period (Moreno, Laje, Blanco et al., 2007). Once considered highly unusual, it would seem the pediatric bipolar disorder was quickly transforming itself into typical childhood mental illness. Moreover, although the population was different, the treatment was more often the same treatment being prescribed to adults. Believing pediatric treatment ought to model adult treatment for the same condition, children were regularly being prescribed off market atypical antipsychotic drugs (Chang, 2007); yet, there was no research to point to noting neither the effectiveness of using such drugs with children nor the safety risks associated with such drugs for such a young population.

The 2007 study acknowledge the possibility that, unless an epidemic had gone unnoticed and was being grossly under diagnosed, there was a real possibility this young population was being "misdiagnosed." As subsequent research suggested, the symptoms of bipolar disorder did not present in the same way for children as symptoms did for adults. Perhaps clinicians were mistaking pediatric bipolar for something else. As Spittler explains, some of the most commonly reported symptoms including "distractibility, pressured speech, and irritability" were overlapping with ADHD (2007, p. 23). While, others argued the differences in symptoms were rooted in developmental differences between children and adults (Chang, 2007); although, the disorder was the same. Being mindful 60% of children being seen by a physician when the precipitating factors for the office visit were symptoms of pediatric bipolar disorder were leaving with prescriptions for multiple drugs (The Brown University Child & Psychopharmacology Update, 2014), it was vital for this concern to be addressed.

With the release of the DSM-5, a new childhood disorder appeared, *disruptive mood dysregulation disorder* (DMDD). At the core of the new condition is "chronic, severe persistent irritability" (American Psychiatric Association, 2013, p. 156) manifesting in "temper outbursts" and prolong mood states of agitation and/or anger. Bipolar disorder is now considered an inappropriate diagnosis for a child between 6 and 18 years of age. Although the diagnostic

BiPolar→DMDD

label has changed from bipolar to DMDD, not much else has changed. Children are still primarily treated with atypical antipsychotics as the drug of choice. The concern expressed by Moreno et al. (2007) for a 400% increase in the number of children being diagnosed has not been sufficiently addressed merely by changing the name of the label.

Anti-psychiatry advocates see the creation of the DMDD label as a means for controlling children's behavior and abdicating parental responsibilities onto a fictitious disorder. The DMDD label provides a justification to medicate, thereby, sedating the child making behavior more compliant and easy to manage. For instance, children in the foster care system were reported to be as much as 11 times more likely to be prescribed psychotropic drugs than those children not part of the foster care system (dos Reis, Zito, Safer et al., 2001). Fontanella, Hiance, Phillips et al. (2014) found that for children the likelihood of being prescribed a psychotropic drug also increased when the child was male, disabled and eligible for Medicaid.

Stigma Inoculation

Being sick (physical or psychological) is a form of social deviance, and adopting a diagnostic label is a means by which society sanctions one's ability to abdicate the social stain and tarnish referred to as *deviance*. At least this is what sociologist Talcott Parsons suggests with his concept of the *sick role*. Suppose, for instance, a single mother of two was in a car accident breaking both her legs now needing to be in bed with both legs in traction for the next four weeks. She asks her parents if they might look after her two young children as she is unable to meet their basic needs: feeding, bathing and dressing. Still, the role of mother requires parents to meet such needs of their children, not doing so constitutes an act of deviance. Contrast this example against another single mother who asks her parents to look after her children for the next four weeks while she goes on a tear of drugging and boozing for a month. In each scenario, children's needs cannot be met by their mother. But in the first, example, if the mother accepts the label of being *sick*, she can relinquish the social stain of being a degenerate, immoral human being while at the same time being excused of her motherly duties. In such instances the diagnosis serves as a means of scrubbing the social stigma away. With a bona fide label of being *sick*, one is excused from going into work necessitating colleagues pick up the slack, going to school requiring the teacher to extend the assignment's due date and postponing the garage from being cleaned up until the next weekend all while maintaining an intact positive social identity.

Parson's sick role also applies to mental illness. The bipolar college student might be granted a complete medical withdraw and tuition refund while being hospitalized for treatment; the schizophrenic patient may be forgiven for rude and insulting comments made while intoxicated by delusional ideas. Having a label of a mental illness provides a secondary benefit to the patient by maintaining an intact social identity. Such secondary gain may incentivize the labeling of otherwise questionable behaviors as "disease." Consider the college student who calls his professor on a Monday afternoon apologizing for missing the morning's class along with the exam. The student, however, explains to the professor that he had a "slip" over the weekend, and he was still too intoxicated to make it to class that morning. He has already attended an AA meeting and met with his AA sponsor. The student is clear, "Please excuse me because I'm an alcoholic." Yet, a second student calls the same professor explaining he just got way too carried away at a keg party over the weekend and was "too messed up" on Monday morning for the class and the exam. Although each student's behavior is similar, one is asking to benefit from the sick role. In the absence of empirical evidence demonstrating an actual corruption or invasion of the body, perhaps, applying the label "disease" to behaviors such as excessive drinking, gambling or sex is merely attempting to assist the individual in acquiring the social benefits of the sick role.

There is a cost which accompanies the sick role label. For many patients who have been diagnosed with a formal label of abnormal, the diagnosis begins to morph into a primary identity. The process, as David Karp (1996) explains, is much like the socialization of what often occurs with career identity. Just as the vocational titles of physician, teacher or lawyer—for many—become a means by which self-identity is understood and social reality is constructed around, so too does the abnormal label. A transformation at some point begins to occur for the patient where he or she begins view their "self" as something other than what it once was believed to be. All events, social interactions and personal behaviors are now understood within the context of this new status of "abnormal," and there is no going back.

The specific diagnostic label (i.e., depressed, ADHD or schizophrenic) provided by the psychotherapist now equips the patient with a new vocabulary. The language that was once absent is now present for naming the problem, and armed with a new vocabulary, the patient sets out to reinterpret their history. "A huge cognitive shift occurs when people come to see that the problem may be internal instead of situational" (Karp, 1996, p. 59). Often the patient, who had chalked up their personal challenges to having unpleasant childhoods, malevolent bosses or an unloving spouse comes to realize that the real problem lied within their "self." The fault was theirs. An entire life history is re-appraised.

The career transformation to becoming an abnormal person is also solidified by making the decision to seek out professional services. Regardless if such services are voluntary or involuntary, it is now public. Even under the umbrella of confidentiality, there is a public recognition of the abnormal label existing, if only between the psychotherapist and patient. For others, however, the public recognition becomes broader when family, friends, teachers or other members of the community are made aware of the abnormal diagnosis. An angry outburst or tearful event by the patient is quickly brushed off by others as being part of the diagnosis, rather than authentic to the person. In time, the patient too comes to terms with this alienation, accepting their mood and behavior as part of their new identity.

The use of psychotropic medication may also contribute to forging this new identity of abnormal. As the patient grapples with medication side-effects that may include—for antidepressants—weight gain, loss of sexual desire, fatigue, limited range of emotional expression and insomnia, he or she may come to feel their authentic self is not the one experiencing life. Often the question asked, "Is this me, or is it my medication?" "Psychiatric drugs add another layer to the search for self because they influence our feelings and moods. They alter our consciousness, and in so doing, they potentially refashion who we believe ourselves to be" (Karp, 2006, p. 97).

This process of identity transformation is not one directional. Just as the patient may come to view himself or herself as an abnormal patient, society at large orientates a social definition towards the patient as well. This new definition is often based on *social stigma*, referring to a deep social disapproval and devaluing of the labeled person. The stigmatized person is, second-class, a social outcast who needs to be avoided and banned from public. In the past, the label of mental illness carried with it significant social stigma, as mental illness was believed to result from personal and moral weakness. Today, this is less the case, but social stigma still exists for the mentally ill. Many people who have been diagnosed with a DSM-5 label fear their employment would be placed in jeopardy should their supervisor find out. Some students fear they must lie on applications to medical schools or law schools when asked if they have ever been treated for a mental illness, raising the question why such professional schools feel the need to ask such questions on admission applications in the first place (Liebert, 2003).

## Pathologicalizing the Normal

If it were one's objective to manufacture more psychopathology, a logical approach for doing so would be to simply redefine that which was once considered to be "normal" as now being "abnormal," to just switch the label as effortlessly as Igor does in the movie *Young Frankenstein* with the two jars containing the "normal" and "Abnormal" brains. One possible method for doing just this is to refocus the clinician's attention away from evaluating the patient's social and physical environment as a confounding factor influencing his or her symptoms. Horwitz and Wakefield (2007) suggest in *The Loss of Sadness*, the shift in the DSM-III (published in 1980) focused now on exclusively diagnosing depression based on symptoms, failing to consider any broader social context. "In other words, its criteria specified the symptoms that must be present to justify a given diagnosis but ignored any reference to the context in which they developed. In so doing, they allowed normal response to stressors to be characterized as symptoms of disorder" (p. viii), resulting in the incidence of depression-related disorders soring to record highs starting in the 1980s. Moreover, new to the DSM-5 (published in 2013) is the discontinuation of the multi-axial system of diagnosing a patient that required factors such as other medical conditions, psycho-social-stressors and the ability of the patient to carryout daily functioning be considered in addition to the clinician's diagnosis of a primary psychopathology.

Consider, for example, many young college students pursuing a degree today. There are few commodities that have increased in price well exceeding the rate of inflation as has college tuition. Many students "suffer" to pursue a degree today. They forego sleep, eat poorly, abandon all prospects for leisure time and work countless hours outside of class lecture time. After a semester or two, such students are fatigued, feel helpless and cringe at their self-worth as they look towards another semester of the same routine. Based on the DSM-5, such students by the start of their junior year are meeting the necessary criteria to be diagnosed with a persistent depressive disorder (PDD). But, are such students depressed, and shouldn't their self-sacrifice be taken into consideration by the evaluating clinician when considering a PDD diagnosis? Viktor Frank referred to despair as "suffering without meaning." In the above vignette, the meaning to such suffering is obvious and offers context to appreciate and understand the symptomology where the troubled student isn't depressed, rather navigating through a "rough patch" in life's journey.

As the diagnostic categories of the DSM have expanded with its revised editions over the decades, a closer analysis of newly included DSM pathology suggests such a possibility for manufacturing psychopathology by reinterpreting "normal" behavior as now being "abnormal." This has been but one argument in opposition to the American Psychiatric Association's adoption of premenstrual dysphoric disorder (PMDD) in the lasted DSM edition under the category of Depressive Disorders. It's estimated that prevalence for PMDD may be as high as 5.8% of all menstruating women where symptoms during most of her menstrual cycles include: mood swings, sadness, increased interpersonal conflicts, self-deprecating thoughts, feeling keyed up, decrease interest in typical activities, change in sleep patterns, change in appetite, fatigued and possible physical symptoms (i.e., breast tenderness, sensation of bloating or joint/muscle pain) (American Psychiatric Association, 2013). Based on these symptoms, it might be argued that once having a menstrual cycle was considered a normal biological phenomenon for women, but now the same biological cycle may be considered abnormal for women to experience. [*handwritten: ~ S4FU DSMS*]

Max Webber, one of sociology's founding fathers, argued the creation of the bureaucracy was one of society's greatest contributions to the Twentieth-Century. The bureaucracy provided an organizational means for efficiently processing a vast number of human needs. Yet, one of his chief concerns with it was the risk—rather than serving humanity—it would be humanity in the end serving the bureaucracy. The American Psychological Association began its organization with just 31 members in 1892, that number rose to 7,272 members by 1950, and 39,411 members in 1975, and now supports 77,5050 members (American Psychological Association, n.d.). The American Psychiatric Association reports an annual revenue stream nearing $85 million (2013b). These two organizations represent the two largest professional organizations serving mental health practice today, and every year they become larger. As Webber suggested the work within bureaucracies always seems to expand to meet the growing size of the organization. Perhaps this organizational trend might offer some possible insight as to the increasing incidence of mental illness within our society today.

# 7 Mrs. Sullivan: A Case Study

Occasionally I still do some forensic consulting, and it was some time back in July, 2016 my wife had a referral for me. I wouldn't be able to meet with my actual client, Mrs. Sullivan, as she was under lock and key in a nearby psychiatric hospital under an order of involuntary examination. Instead, I first met with her daughter, Anna, who was an attorney and would be responsible for paying my fee. She was quite distraught, and at first I found myself distracted wondering how it was that she could instill a sense of confidence in her own clients remembering my wife telling me she was "a fine trial attorney." She rambled and wasn't telling me everything I needed to know. Not my typical approach, nevertheless, I found myself interrupting her in midsentence and asking very direct questions. As the information was coming to me in a more logical fashion, a picture of events was beginning to take shape.

Five days earlier an emergency room physician had signed an *Involuntary Psychiatric Examination* order for Mrs. Sullivan. All states have statutes governing the process of ensuring emergency psychiatric care is offered in the event a patient is in crisis demonstrating a clear danger to self and/or others. In the state where I'm licensed, such an order may be initiated by a licensed mental health professional, physician or law enforcement officer. Once signed, the patient must be escorted by the police to the nearest psychiatric facility to be evaluated by either a clinical psychologist or psychiatrist. Should the evaluation determine the patient continues to pose a danger to self and/or others, the hospital will petition the court for a legal hearing, and the patient will continue to stay in the hospital until the time of the hearing; otherwise, the patient must be discharged within 72 hours. Once again, Mrs. Sullivan's admission was now in the fifth day, well past 72 hours. Moreover, the hospital was offering little information to either Anna or her father.

Each day since Mrs. Sullivan's admission, Anna and her father signed into the hospital's guest log, left their personal belongings (i.e., cell phones) in a locker, passed through a metal detector and were escorted one at a time to the visiting room. Mrs. Sullivan refused to see either her husband or daughter. "Why wouldn't she see us? Does she give you a reason?" Anna would ask each time before being told she had to leave the visiting room. "Patients have the right to refuse visitors. They don't need to give us a reason. They have rights you know," the nurse would simply say in response. Anna looked straight at me as if I were one of the juries she was making her final argument to; "you have to help me get my mother out of this place!" Then she added, "It's a real shit hole."

When patients (or their family members) are distraught, they will tell you information that seems important to them but not at all helpful to me. I didn't need to know Anna was conceived when Mrs. Sullivan was a junior in high school and a shotgun wedding followed. I did need to know, however, there had been a long history of depression. Mrs. Sullivan's depression first started maybe twenty years earlier. Mrs. Sullivan self-medicated with alcohol. There had been a long history of alcoholism as well, but the drinking had stopped about a year before. "She just stopped drinking when she was diagnosed with ovarian cancer. They took both her ovaries and with them her desire to drink," Anna explained to me. The depression, on the other hand, was relentless and burrowed deep into her life; that she couldn't seem to shake. "She's mean... I mean the depression makes her so mean... and nasty too. When I talk about her to other people, I refer to her as the 'dragon.'"

Their family doctor had prescribed the antidepressant Zoloft (at 50 mg.) about a year ago, about the time she had stopped drinking. The Zoloft seemed to be having little if any effect for Mrs. Sullivan who refused over-and-over again to talk with a psychotherapist about her depression. "I did some research and found some articles suggesting for older adults Abilify might be helpful in her treatment," Anna explained to me. Reluctantly, her mother agreed to allow Anna to attend her next doctor's appointment. She brought photocopies of the research articles touting the benefits of Abilify along with her, and Mrs. Sullivan left the appointment with a prescription for the new drug (at 5 mg.). Abilify is an atypical, antipsychotic medication that is used sometimes at low dosages to augment the treatment for major depression.

"I couldn't believe how well it was working. She was now actually pleasant to talk to and be around. She was even smiling, something I hadn't seen in years. I thought Abilify was a magical drug!" Anna explained to me. Then she became very serious losing all affect in her face as she began to describe the events that unfolded just five days before when she received a frantic phone call from her father. "'She's gone crazy!' That's all my father would say to me. Over and over, he just kept saying, 'She's gone crazy!' I could hear my mom in the background screaming. She was making no sense whatsoever. 'One, two, three, four, FOUR, FOUR, FOURRRR!' I'm telling you it made no sense. I could hear her yelling out how she wanted all her blood donated to the Salvation Army," Anna said to me. Although

Anna pleaded with her father to call an ambulance, he refused saying it would cost too much money; somehow he got Mrs. Sullivan into their car and drove her the emergency room. Anna arrived about 15 minutes later.

The nurse was in the room asking what medications Mrs. Sullivan was taking when Anna finally found her way back to examination room. Mr. Sullivan had been smart enough to bring all the pill bottles with him in a plastic zip lock bag: Crestor (e.g., cholesterol), Lisinopril (e.g., high blood pressure) and Zoloft (e.g., depression). "What about Abilify? She's still taking Abilify?" Anna asked her dad. He didn't refill the prescription pointing out that it was costing over $300 for a month's supply. The nurse's face gave it away. Anna didn't understand the risks associated with abruptly stopping an antipsychotic, but she understood all at once from the nurse's look, this was the problem. Just then the ER physician entered the room to which Mrs. Sullivan began yelling, "'you just crawled out of my dog's ass!'"

In just a few minutes, the ER doctor was speaking privately to both Anna and Mr. Sullivan out in the hallway. He suspected Mrs. Sullivan was suffering from an abrupt discontinuation of her antipsychotic medication which is a known concern. Antipsychotic medication cannot just be stopped. Patients need to be gradually taken off the medication under the close observation by the prescribing psychopharmacologist; otherwise, there is a risk of psychosis occurring. Nevertheless, the ER doctor needed to take some blood and urine from Mrs. Sullivan to ensure that something else was not the cause of her psychosis, although he thought this to be unlikely. There was problem; Mrs. Sullivan was refusing to give up her blood and urine for analysis. If she keeps refusing, the doctor explained, the family's permission would be needed for an Involuntary Psychiatric Examination (IPE) to be initiated.

There is nearly nothing more invasive and restrictive than an IPE. It is a tool psychotherapists have at their disposal, and sadly it is a tool oftentimes used incorrectly, as I believe was the case for Mrs. Sullivan. Lots of time is spent filling up the hours in graduate classrooms on patients' rights to decline care and even opt for suicide, but in the real world of actual clinical practice such questions are mute. Psychotherapists have an ethical obligation to ensure no such harm falls knowingly on their patient or others around them. Significant harm (meaning mortal injury) to self or others is not ever an option. Psychotherapists must intervene, and initiating an IPE is just one option a psychotherapist must have at the ready should such circumstance present. Still, an IPE is one of the most invasive and restrictive forms of intervention. By initiating an IPE, the psychotherapist is removing all rights endowed upon an adult. Unlike the police who have arrested a person and taken him or her into custody, no crime had been committed; yet, a person's constitutional rights are being revoked while undesired care and custody is being imposed.

Too often IPEs are used to protect the psychotherapist (or in the case of Mrs. Sullivan, a physician). The psychotherapist who is concerned about the possible risks of personal litigation overreacts and uses the IPE. In such instances, the psychotherapist wants to clearly document that a life has been protected at all cost. Just because a patient's behavior warrants the use of an IPE doesn't mean that IPE is necessary. Ethically, psychotherapists must suggest the least restrictive and least invasive means of intervention first. In the instance of concern over suicide risk, for example, the psychotherapist might consider the use of a *Suicide Contract*[7] before the use of IPE. In the case of Mrs. Sullivan,

---

[7] The psychotherapist has a patient who he or she believes is at "risk" for committing suicide sign a contract promising he or she

she had already been involuntarily sedated, which was appropriate intervention by the physician under such circumstances. Moreover, her husband consented to the sedation, as a spouse may consent to a medical treatment at such time the other spouse is incapacitated to make such a decision for one's self. I suspect, in this case, the physician was concerned Mrs. Sullivan's psychosis would persist once the sedation lost its hold placing him in a difficult position concerning eventual discharge. The IPE ensured a seamless discharge transition from emergency room to the psychiatric hospital just down the street. The ER doctor may also assume this would ensure Mrs. Sullivan would receive sufficient follow-up mental health care.

The ER physician also erred by asking the family for their permission to initiate the IPE. This is—unfortunately—also typical since family cannot consent or decline an IPE. Only a physician, licensed psychotherapist or law enforcement officer can sign the IPE. Moreover, family/spouse/best friend's consent is not necessary. The IPE is based entirely on the professional opinion of the professional signing the IPE. Yet, the psychotherapist may ask for family's consent as if to suggest they too are owning the responsibility for the events that will shortly follow.

---

will refrain from harming themselves for a specified time-period (i.e., the next two weeks). In the meantime, the patient agrees to meet with the psychotherapist three or four times over the course of the week, will call an emergency suicide hotline outside of normal office hours, or report to the nearest emergency room and ask for the on-call psychiatrist. Suicide contracts are considered appropriate interventions when there is elevated risk but not severe risk based on a proper suicide risk-evaluation. Use of an IPE when there is not severe risk—based on community standards of practice and care—is consider to be excessive.

The following morning, Mrs. Sullivan was transported a few miles down the street to a psychiatric hospital. In those five days, she had not spoken to her family refusing their visits and phone calls. The 72 hours had passed, and a reasonable assumption could be made the psychiatric hospital had made a petition to the court requesting a hearing to determine extended hospitalization. Anna, her daughter, was now asking how I might be able to assist in getting her mother discharged from the facility.

The role of a forensic expert is clear. He or she is being engaged to share expert opinion, not to provide care and treatment. For this reason, I tend to refer to those I provide forensic assessment to as *clients* and those who I provide psychotherapy to as *patients*. Moreover, with forensic assessments, the scope of the "opinion" also needs to be clearly operationalized. What is the actual opinion being sought? For Mrs. Sullivan, the question at hand was the necessity for continued psychiatric hospitalization. If the facility was petitioning the court to grant continued involuntary hospitalization, the burden of proof was that such care could not be accomplished by less restive means or in a less restrictive care setting. The forensic expert, unlike an attorney, is not an advocate for the person consulting for their opinion. A forensic expert should not slant their opinion to serve the interest of their client over that of the psychological truth of the matter. Finally, serving as a forensic expert requires consent. In some instances, the court may appoint a forensic expert. In the instance of Mrs. Sullivan, I would require her consent to serve in this capacity. At this point, I did not have such consent.

I left this initial meeting with Anna letting her know I wasn't going to be able to serve as a forensic expert and assess Mrs. Sullivan's needs for involuntary psychiatric care without either a court order or her mother's consent. The lines between psychotherapist and forensic expert can be clearly differentiate at one level yet blur at other levels. I suggested first thing the next morning she needed to get aggressive with the hospital leaving no doubt in their minds that she was a ferocious trial attorney, and they would rather wrestle a hungry alligator right out to a Florida swamp than deal with her. She needed to know why her mother was refusing to speak with her or have an opportunity to speak with her mother immediately. As an attorney, Anna understood that experts have limitations and can't work miracles. As she left my office with her hand on the door knob, she asked me, "Do you know where my father was when my mother was told she had cancer last year? .... At the dog track!"

Anna called me the next morning. It was about 11:00 a.m. "Guess where I am?" Like many lawyers I've known, she preferred to answer her own questions, "I'm at the hospital with mom." Anna had convinced the Director of Nursing to simply ask Mrs. Sullivan why she was refusing to communicate with her family. A novel idea, yet still not negating Mrs. Sullivan's right to refuse such visits. Apparently, Mrs. Sullivan was under the false impression both her husband and daughter had her committed to the hospital, not for short term care but for permanent placement. I later learned this was a threat oftentimes made by her husband back when she was actively drinking. When the nurse told her she was mistaken, in fact, her daughter was trying desperately to get her discharged, the tide turned and within an hour Anna was meeting with her mother. Anna was permitted unrestricted access to meet with her mother once she flashed her bar license and declared herself to be her mother's attorney[8]. Now serving in this capacity, Anna could consent for me to have access to provide a forensic evaluation of capacity to determine Mrs. Sullivan's need for continued involuntary psychiatric hospitalization. I arrived to the facility later that day.

The evaluation involved a review of her medical record, with most of my time being used to decipher the psychiatrist's handwriting. I was concerned his diagnosis suggested psychosis, rather than a substance/medication-induced psychotic disorder[9]. The abrupt discontinuation of the Abilify was the most logical explanation for the psychotic symptoms witnessed in the emergency room. I also met with Mrs. Sullivan to evaluate her capacity. Although she demonstrated some minor challenges with short-term memory, her other executive functioning appeared intact. When I offered to schedule her an appointment with both a psychiatrist and psychologist following her discharge, she said, "I don't want any of that." Anna who was present during my evaluation said, "If you let Dr. Liebert set up these appointments for you, it will help you get out of here

---

[8] In the state of Florida, psychiatric hospitals must provide patients access to a public use phone, offer opportunities for visitation with family and/or friends. Such visitation is typically restricted to no more than one designated hour each day and just one person at a time may visit. However, the hospital must allow unrestricted, private access to the patient's attorney and clergy.

[9] Substance/medication-induced psychotic disorder is an appropriate diagnosis when there are psychotic symptoms present (i.e., delusions and hallucinations) but there is also evidence these symptoms developed "during or soon after substance intoxication or withdrawal or after exposure to a medication. [Moreover,] the involved substance/medication is capable of producing the symptoms…" (American Psychiatric Association, 2013, p. 110). Differentiating an accurate diagnosis is vital in this instance as it also significantly influences appropriate treatment decisions.

sooner. We want to show the doctors here at this hospital we have proper care waiting for you when you leave." Mrs. Sullivan immediately consented demonstrating her insight and ability to make informed decisions. My assessment ended by accomplishing the following: first, I could professionally determine Mrs. Sullivan no longer posed a danger to herself or others. Second, she could participate in making decisions about her own care. Third, we could set up an immediate discharge plan that was both safe and effective in a less restrictive location. My next step was calling the treating psychiatrist and request he order an immediate discharge.

I got lucky and the phone call wasn't necessary. A nurse came into the conference room where I had been meeting with Mrs. Sullivan alerting me that her psychiatrist was in the facility checking on his patients. I caught his attention in the hallway letting him know immediately I had been appointed by Mrs. Sullivan's attorney to conduct an IME[10]; this caught his complete attention. I explained I did not see any evidence of dangerousness and shared the aftercare program we had already put into place for her, the psychiatrist said, "Mrs. Sullivan is a nice lady. I think it's best she stays until the hearing," which was scheduled for the day after next. I may have made an error in judgement by using such language as "IME" and "no evidence of dangerousness." I was attempting to let the psychiatrist know, without directly saying so, that lawyers are now involved, and it would be in everyone's best interest to discharge his patient now, but—as is sometimes the case—my informal message was received as a challenge to his authority, and he was now

---

[10] An Independent Medical Examination (IME) refers to an assessment typically conducted in forensic cases where it is likely the court is going to hear opposing diagnoses and treatment recommendations.

going to see Mrs. Sullivan's stay was stretched out if he could manage to stretch it out.

Anna was furious. "There's no way I'm going to let mom stay here another night. This is all my father's fault, and I'm going to fix this mess he made. I want her discharged immediately!" My role as a forensic expert is to, first ensure that I do not compromise neither the ethics nor integrity of the profession. Second, I need to meet the needs of the client. Psychiatric hospitals are unpleasant as the food is unappetizing, socks are standard footwear since they are san shoelaces and there is little to do to pass the time that crawls at a snail's pace. Yet, neither is Ken Kessey's portrayal of psychiatric hospitals in *One Flew Over the Cuckoo's Nest* an actuate portrayal either. Although I appreciated Anna's frustration over the situation, the situation was not dire either. After five days, Mrs. Sullivan could certainly survive another two days. Nevertheless, Anna was indignant that her mother was going to get out as soon as possible. It was now just past 5:00 p.m., and the courts were closed. Nothing was possible tonight. She told me I needed to make myself available first thing in the morning as she was planning on filing an emergency *habeas corpus*[11].

As promised, Anna was at the courthouse, first in line, when the clerk's office opened for business. She secured an emergency hearing for early that afternoon. As requested, I reported to the judge's chambers ready to testify. Mrs. Sullivan was present too, as a *habeas corpus* requires "the body" to be presented to the judge. The treating psychia-

---

[11] A Latin term that translates as "you have the body." A *writ of habeas corpus* requires a government agency or individual to present the prisoner or captive person to a judge for the purpose to determine if their involuntary confinement is in violation of their constitutional rights and immediate release should be ordered.

trist—however—failed to show up for the hearing. My testimony was not necessary. In the absence of the treating psychiatrist, the judge granted the order for *habeas corpus*, and Mrs. Sullivan was discharged from the hospital and was back on her way home just a couple of hours later.

One of the advantages many forensic experts speak of in doing this sort of work is the clear point where the work begins and where it ends. When working with patients (not clients), psychotherapists feel a sense of responsibility for the "whole picture." We are there for the patient to address and process with them all aspects of their life. Moreover, we understand what is discussed in the therapy office flows into all the many pores of their life, and there is a level of stress that accompanies this dimension of the relationship. The forensic relationship, however, is more objectively defined. We are essentially a "tool" for the client, and it can be pleasant at times to only have a limited, clearly defined responsibility for the client. Yet, there is a different sort of stress that accompanies this sort of relationship too. For instance, I believe I was helpful to Mrs. Sullivan, only in that I facilitated her discharge by about 24 hours, and this 24 hours came at great expense and effort. Furthermore, the psychotherapist in me desperately wanted to raise the concerns I was witnessing in the family dynamic with Anna. Her harden determination to see her mother released seemed so clearly fueled by her hostility towards her father. She saw her mother's IPE the result of her father's carelessness, seeing the opportunity to project some of her anger at his callous disregard towards her mother. Our ethics, nevertheless, require that we don't cross roles, either the person paying the fee is a client or they are a patient, but they can't be both.

# 8 Trial by Science

Psychology is a science, an empirical science employing the same scientific method as those engaged in biological, astrological and chemical research. Moreover, this practice of clinical psychology is rooted so deeply in science that one might assume white lab coats are required attire for him or her. This, of course, is of no surprise as the scientific method is introduced in the psychology curriculum right from the start. All introductory textbooks include—typically in the either the first or second chapter—a dedicated discussion outlining the rigors of psychological science. Students are taught how different methodologies yield varying degrees of certainty. Correlational methodologies can demonstrate association but never causation; whereas, experimental methods are the Cadillac of empirical pursuits yielding findings now placing the chicken in front of the egg. With experimentation, we know, "smoking" causes "cancer," not that "cancer" (or those with a genic predisposition for cancer) causes folks to go out and "smoke." We learn in this chapter that qualitative methods favoring use of ethnographies or case studies— which might be highly interesting to read—yield little in the way of meaningful research findings. For those seeking to establish themselves as respected professionals in the field, they should stay away from such research approaches.

Psychologists, however, are not scientists—at least not like chemists, biologists and physicists are scientists. Unlike those just mentioned, psychologists deal with a phenomenon these others don't address: the essence of a human being. Clinical psychologists work with human beings who are downright complex, living confounding lives tangled up alongside other human beings, all while sharing environments as indistinct as the swirls and blots on a Rorschach card. No cosmic consolation or chemical compound is as multifarious as is a human person, meaning the ebb and flow of clinical practice is also influenced by factors other than science. For instance, psychologists craft a practice that—along with scientific findings—is influenced by verdicts. Juries and judges have their say too. For good or bad, the practice of clinical psychology is shaped as litigation, both criminal as well as civil, plays out in the courtrooms of America. One must keep in mind verdicts are not based on an empirical process governed by the scientific method.

As the lights of the disco ball faded and the 1980s began, it was the courts that might have driven the final nail in Freud's coffin. Although dead and cremated decades earlier, his influence lived on as the ultimate authority in the fields of clinical psychology and psychiatry. Psychoanalysts held the keys to control and influence. After all, it was the psychoanalysts who transformed the practice of mental health taking psychoanalysts out of the asylums, relocating them to profitable private practices where their days ended by 5:00 pm. Still, the superiority of psychoanalytic approaches to treatment had long been supported by use of case study methodologies which were understood to be methodologically weak in comparison to correlation or experimental approaches. Psychoanalytic authority was especially being challenged with the use of pharmacological treatments in the recent decades leading up to the 1980s on methodological grounds. The science was simply showing these new medications were more effective than psychoanalysis. Rather than challenging these objectively obtained numbers, the psychoanalytic community jibed in response by emphasizing their subjectively cultivated experience as the basis for their authority suggesting pharmacological approaches to treatment were superficially masking problems that throbbed much deeper in the human psyche.

In January, 1979 Raphael Osheroff, MD admitted himself to Chestnut Lodge which was a residential psychiatric center located in Rockville, Maryland. Osheroff was a 41-year old nephrologist[12] who had a prior treatment history for anxiety and depression. He had been prescribed medications but had not been compliant in taking his medications. Now, two years later, his symptoms had returned along with suicidal thoughts. On this basis, he admitted himself to Chestnut Lodge. This facility, however, embraced a psychoanalytic-only approach to treatment. Once admitted, Osheroff was also diagnosed with a narcissistic personality disorder, suggesting analytic treatment would require about three years of in-patient care. In the months that followed, Osheroff's condition worsens, as his agitation exacerbated, he began compulsively pacing the hallways, developed insomnia and lost over 40 pounds. In September, his parents were successful in getting Osheroff transferred to a different hospital where he received lithium medication for what is now being diagnosed as a psychotic depressive reaction. Within a few weeks, Osheroff's condition improves, and he is discharged from the hospital in November. Upon his discharge, however, Osheroff learns that his medical license has been revoked, he's broke and he's lost custody of his children. In March the following year, he brings a lawsuit against Chestnut Lodge (Osheroff v. Chestnut Lodge, 1980) claiming they had an ethical duty to offer

---

[12] A physician specializing in the treatment of kidney disorders.

Osheroff v. Chestnut Lodge 1980

him a treatment—that in this case would have been medication—empirical evidence demonstrates to be the most ef-
fectual means of treatment. Osheroff prevails in the lawsuit
and an ethical shift follows where mental health professionals have a responsibility now to develop treatment plans for
patients based on validated approaches.

Integrated in graduate training today, psychologists
are taught to development treatment approaches that embrace the integration of evidence-based research. It's not
relevant that one "believes" or "feels" existentialism, hu-
manism, psychodynamic, etc. theories offer the best argument for understanding the workings of the human psyche.
Today, theory must match up to validated treatment outcomes for it to be an excepted treatment approach. This is
not to suggest patients, based on informed consent, can't
opt for talk-based treatment approaches over medication-
based treatments when the research suggests the latter to be
more effective. Moreover, this doesn't mean patients can't
consent to psychoanalysis for gaining greater self-awareness, rather than for treatment of a specific psychopathology. The Osheroff case changed the landscape of practice
in that patients need to express informed consent. A patient
needs to understand both the risks, benefits and alternative
options available to support their treatment. The practice of
clinical psychology has aligned to the medical movement referred to as *evidence-based medicine* (EBM). EBM is driven by
research where one practices as the peer-reviewed journal
suggests.

It just so happened the court's decision in the
Osheroff case sided in favor of science. This isn't always the
case. Consider the basis on which the U.S. Food and Drug
Administration (FDA) in 2004 issued a public warranting
that the use of Selective Serotonin Reuptake Inhibitor
(SSRI) medication by children and adolescents may elevate

risk for suicidal thoughts and behaviors. A couple of years later the risk was extended to all those under the age of 25. All prescriptions of SSRIs today contain a warning label to this effect which is clearly noted on the medication bottle. Yet, the scientific evidence would tend not to support the FDA's decision to require the warning label. The elevated risk for suicidal thoughts and behaviors for this age group, based on the scientific literature, would suggest the cause not to be the SSRI medication, rather factors unrelated to the medication. Caballero and Nahata (2005) suggest two significant factors. First, children's livers don't metabolize SSRIs at the same rate as adults'. The general idea is to pre-scribe children lower dosages of medication, but this may not be the best approach when it comes to SSRIs where the child's liver seems to metabolize the medication at a rate faster than an adult's liver. Since most SSRIs being pre-scribed to children are not being prescribed by pediatric psy-chiatrists, children may not be receiving an effective dosage. Thus, the problem is not with the SSRI. Rather, the problem is with the prescriber. Second, adolescents are known to be notoriously noncompliant with their medications. It's not unusual for a teenager to skip his or her SSRI today because they are feeling good, even made an A on the algebra test, but feel the need to take the medication the next day since they are feeling bad following an argument with a boyfriend or girlfriend. SSRIs require consistency in taking the medi-cation to ensure an effective level of the drug is pulsing through the bloodstream. Too often following a suicide, blood analysis suggests the teenager had not been taking the medication as prescribed.

The FDA's mandate to include a warning label ac-company all SSRI prescriptions for those under 25 years of age was the result of lawsuits. Scientific substantiation is not a requirement to successfully prevail in a lawsuit. Juries may be influenced by the profound emotions of grieving parents. Plaintiff's lawyers regularly engage in a courtroom strategies referred to as the *reptile strategy*. Although most neuropsychologists disagree with the evolutionary science upon which the strategy is based, the goal is to make the jury angry. As feelings of rage begin to rise in the jury, the lawyer then points the finger at the defendant, in this instance who is the pharmaceutical industry. As Marcia Angel, former editor of the *New England Journal of Medicine* explains, "verdicts have little to do with the merits of the case, and everything to do with theater" (1996, p.74). Prior to the FDA's requiring a warning label accompany SSRI prescriptions, the pharmaceutical industry was hit with a litany of multi-million dollar verdicts. The warning label benefits the pharmaceutical industry by helping to insulate them from future lawsuits.

The well-trained psychologist today not only requires robust training in psychotherapy, research methodology, but, sociology as well. The forces contributing to sound psychological practice need to include a solid appreciation of a culture's influence too. Society's institutions, such as the legal system, has its subtle influence on clinical practice too.

# 9 Mentally Ill Accessing Higher Education[13]

The diagnosis of a mental illness is a powerful social label. For those diagnosed, the social stigma of mental illness too frequently becomes a master status. Not only do many in society look at the mentally ill with moral disgust, hostility, and fear, but also for those diagnosed there is often the reality of social isolation, an absence of self-esteem, and a bleak outlook for the future (Link & Phelan, 1999). Perhaps the true strength of this stigmatizing label is witnessed best at that time the patient becomes asymptomatic. The stigmatizing effects of mental illness can long out live the disorder itself. Not all forms of mental illness represent lifelong conditions. Mental illness can resolve. Moreover, many types of mental illness do not render the patient completely dysfunctional. Some people who suffer from mental illness function at relatively high levels especially when following through with an ongoing treatment plan.

Those who once suffered from mental illness or must manage and control their psychiatric symptoms face intimidating obstacles in their effort to become reintegrated back into mainstream society (Link & Phelan, 1999). Bearing in mind many forms of major mental illness such as schizophrenia often manifest initially in late adolescence or

---

[13] Original publication: Liebert, D. (2003). Access to higher education for the mentally ill: A review of trends, implications, and future possibilities for the Americans with Disability Act and the Rehabilitation Act. *The International Journal of Psychosocial Rehabilitation, 7,* 89-100.

the early 20s, it would seem logical that for many former mental patients the process of reestablishing a healthy life would include the pursuit of formal higher education. Higher education is a socially accepted means by which we pursue our life goals and meaningfully participate as productive members in society. Yet, the walls within higher education do not readily offer sanctuary for the mentally ill from the stigma of their condition. "Mental health service providers may not be providing these individuals with support for their educational endeavors" (Mowbray & Megivern, 1999, p. 32).

It is the purpose of this paper to point out that for the asymptomatic mental patient and former mental patient access to the world of higher education poses yet one more obstacle. The institution of higher education reflects the larger society; it is a microcosm for the larger society. We will find within it the same values, beliefs and prejudices that we find in society as a whole. This paper will explore the legal standards established by the courts and policies of higher education in addressing issues of admission and access for the asymptomatic patient and former mental patient. Specifically, this paper will explore the legal protections afforded to the mentally ill in seeking access to higher education by reviewing the 1973 Rehabilitation Act and by reviewing the Americans with Disabilities Act. This paper will go on to analyze how the courts have interpreted these protections for the asymptomatic and former mental patient by reviewing several contemporary federal court cases. Finally, recommendations for potential policy revision and reform will be offered.

The Rehabilitation Act and the Americans with Disabilities
Act: How it ought to be
Students with disabilities, such as mental illness,
who are otherwise able to meet the criteria for admission
and academic performance are afforded various protections
in the United States under two pieces of federal legislation:
The Rehabilitation Act of 1973 and the Americans with Disabilities Act. These two acts collectively help to ensure that
institutions of higher education make reasonable accommodations to those with disabilities by using federal funding as
political leverage. In this section, we will briefly explore the
foundation and purpose for each of these two federal acts.
With its passage in 1973, the Rehabilitation Act
(RA) required that all postsecondary institutions receiving
federal funding make their programs accessible to those students with disabilities. Institutions that participated in federal funding programs were now prohibited from denying
access to students with disabilities. Such access did not,
however, apply to all students with any disability. Rather, it
applied to those with a "qualifying handicap." As the RA
states:

> No qualified handicapped student shall, on the basis of
> handicap, be excluded from participation in, be denied
> the benefits of, other otherwise be subjected to discrim-
> ination under any academic, research, occupation train-
> ing, housing, health insurance, counseling, financial aid,
> physical education, athletics, recreation, transportation,
> other extracurricular, or other postsecondary education
> aid, benefits, or services to which this subpart applies.
> (§104.42)

This concept of a "qualified handicap" was clearly defined
in the landmark Supreme Court Case of *Southern Community
College v. Davis*. Ms. Davis, a nursing student, was denied

continued admission in her clinical nursing program because she was deaf. The community college she attended believed that her hearing disability posed a safety risk to patients and there was no "reasonable" means for the disability to be accommodated. Ms. Davis sued and the community college initially prevailed. Ms. Davis appealed the decision, and the higher court then found in Ms. Davis' favor. The court ruled that Southeastern Community College must evaluate Ms. Davis without consideration of her disability. The college appealed to the United States Supreme Court. The Court was essentially being asked to decide if "otherwise qualified" means that one can perform despite the disability or that the disability may not be considered in assessing the candidate's propensity to perform in the academic program. The Court ruled that "An otherwise qualified person is one who is able to meet all of the programs requirements despite his handicap" (*Southeastern Community College v. Davis*, 1979, p. 406).

Therefore, institutions may deny access to the disabled if their disability inhibits their ability to reasonably complete the course of study, but not if the disability can be reasonably accommodated for rendering the student "otherwise" able to perform. For instance, a technical college could deny admission into a dental hygienic program to a blind student because there exists no reasonable way to accommodate for the disability. But, admission could not be denied to the same student into a history department because the disability could be reasonably accommodated. Reasonable accommodations may include, for instance, having books read onto tape, classroom note-takers, use of tape recorders, or the use of service animals.

With the passage of the Americans with Disabilities Act (ADA) in 1991, the implications of the RA were broadened. Title II of the ADA not only applies to schools receiving federal funding, but it also applies to all public entities regardless if they receive such funding. The ADA also expresses broader goals. As McGovern (1992) explains, the ADA is motivated by two far-reaching goals. First, it is the intention of the ADA to advance a primary goal of eliminating the stigma and discrimination too frequently associated with disability. Second, the ADA expresses the goal of minimizing the impact of a disability on a person by maximizing the person's growth and development as an autonomous person.

Clearly then it has been established that students cannot be discriminated against simply due to a handicap. Moreover, this same argument applies to those with mental illness as well (Stefan, 2001). In other words, postsecondary institutions cannot deny access to higher education programs merely due to a student's psychological disability. Schools, of course, may deny access if the student's mental disability cannot be reasonably accommodated for. For instance, if a student suffering with schizophrenia is actively experiencing psychosis and is acting dangerously to himself or others, he may be denied access. As Alikhan explains, "A person who poses a 'direct threat' to the health or safety of others will not be considered a 'qualified person' with a disability" (2001, p. 165). In contrast, however, a student being treated for schizophrenia with the use of antipsychotic medication may experience significant uncontrollable tremors of his or her hands. Providing the use of a tape recorder or note-taker for class lectures and discussions could reasonably accommodate for such side-effects.

In summary, those with mental illness are afforded the same protections under RA and ADA as others suffering from physical disabilities. However, as we will come to see, institutions of higher education do not apply the RA and ADA as vigorously to those with mental illness as is applied to those with a physical disability. Not all forms of disability are equally stigmatizing.

Higher Education and Accessibility for the Mentally Ill

In some respects, higher education has been rather distinguished in its employment of accessibility for the mentally ill. As Stefan (2001) points out, academia has been forthcoming in making reasonable accommodations in several respects. For instance, many students with diagnosed learning disabilities and other recognized disabilities such as attention deficit hyperactivity disorder are granted increased time for examinations; classroom note-takers aid students in getting the professor's lecture down on paper, and by providing private testing environments, students are better able to manage the distractions or anxieties brought about by their psychological conditions. In addition, institutions of higher education are now readily omitting from admissions application questions concerning mental health history. Asking a student what sort of psychological disorders he or she has been treated for is no longer appropriate, or necessary admissions data. These are certainly positive changes from the perspective of those with mental health disabilities. Clearly, some of the walls have been broken down.

Higher education, however, is also a social institution within a much larger society, and as a social institution, higher education represents a microcosm of the larger society. We can see within this institution ethnocentric reflections of what is believed to be right and wrong, just and unjust, and we can find expressed the prejudices the mentally ill face in the larger society as well. Despite several

gains, higher education has at the same time maintained un-
due challenges and obstacles for the mentally ill in their
quest for access to higher education. We can see these challenges evolve out of the civil litigation brought by students
seeking relief from the courts under the RA and ADA. In
this section, we will examine several contemporary civil
cases and explore the implications of accessibility for the
mentally ill.

Doe v. New York University: U.S. Court of Appeals,
Second Circuit (1981)
　　　Doe, a medical student at New York University
(NYU), sought legal intervention from the court because
she was denied readmission to NYU due to a psychiatric
disability. Does suffered from borderline personality disorder. On appeal, the Supreme Court found in Doe's favor.
　　　Jane Doe's mental health history begins in childhood with several questionable instances of pathological
events. The Court's opinion cites that in the third grade,
Doe had trouble with her grade school teacher that resulted
in some sort of intervention with a psychologist. At the age
of 14, there was another mental health intervention by a psychiatrist who treated Doe after she and her parents had an
argument, and Doe attempted suicide by taking five sleeping
pills. These isolated descriptions noted in the Court's opinion was not sufficient to confirm any presence of childhood
psychopathology.
　　　In Doe's early to mid-20s, her pathology appears
more established. Prior to her application to medical school
in 1975, there are several events that clearly call her mental
status into question. Specifically, there were several inci-
dents where she caused significant physical harm to herself—although it is not stated that these attempts were actual suicide attempts. For instance, she cut herself several

times, and on one occasion the self-inflicted injury necessitated a blood transfusion. She violently—but not lethally—attacked several of her psychologists and psychiatrists. These behaviors resulted in several psychiatric hospitalizations. It is also important to point out that these assaults took place when Doe's psychologists were attempting to involuntarily commit her.

Despite her psychological difficulties, Doe could be able to make application to medical school. The Court's opinion does not speak of her undergraduate accomplishments, but it stands to reason Doe must have completed her undergraduate degree with some level of success, could earn a respectable score on her medical school admissions examination, and secure encouraging letters of recommendation to be accepted by NYU. NYU admitted Doe in 1975 to pursue the M.D. degree.

Doe's accomplishments, however, were not all honestly stated. In her application, she falsely represented "...that she did not then have and had not had any chronic or recurrent illness or emotional problems" (*Doe v. New York University*, 1981, p. 766). As part of the entrance requirement upon starting her first year's classes, Doe was required to complete a medical physical by a physician representing the university. Upon her physical examination, the doctor noticed several scars from Doe's previous self-injurious activities. It was now, Doe acknowledged her mental health past. This admission prompted the university to require Doe to undergo a more thorough mental health evaluation.

Upon the completion of her psychiatric evaluation, the university initially recommended that Doe withdraw from the university. Doe objected, and the university agreed to allow Doe to purse her medical training if she "...undertake psychiatric therapy with a medical follow-up by the Student Health Service. Doe accepted these conditions and was advised that if she had further psychiatric trouble she would be expected to withdraw from the school" (*Doe v. New York University*, 1981, p. 766). Further psychiatric trouble occurred soon after when Doe bled herself with the aid of a catheter as a means of dealing with stress. A leave of absence was given.

Doe left New York and returned to California where she began psychiatric treatment by a team of two psychiatrists. In July of 1977, Doe made application for readmission back to NYU medical school. Both of her treating psychiatrists provided positive letters of recommendation to NYU on Doe's behalf. NYU denied her request.

In short, the university claimed that Doe suffered from a psychological condition known as borderline personality disorder (BPD). Furthermore, BPD is a condition that responds poorly to treatment; thus, there was little hope that she would be able to fully overcome her illness. Any duration of time where Doe was asymptomatic merely reflected a dawdling in her condition. It would only be a matter of time, the university feared, before she would become symptomatic again.

In response to NYU's decision, in October of 1977, Doe sought legal intervention for being reinstated in the medical program. Doe claimed that she had been denied readmission because of a disability that was in direct violation of the 1973 Rehabilitation Act. Schools receiving federal funding are not permitted to deny access to a candidate on the mere basis of a disability. On September 25, 1981, Judge Goettel ruled that NYU had in fact denied Doe's readmission based on her disability. The judge stated in his opinion:

> [Ms. Doe would] ... more than likely than not be able to complete her course of medical studies and serve creditably as a physician...[and] NYU had failed to sustain its burden of going forward and proving Doe was not an

> otherwise qualified handicapped person or that her application for readmission was rejected for reasons other than her handicap. (*Doe v. New York University*, 1981, p. 772-773)

Doe returned to NYU medical school in October of 1981.

The Doe case establishes several important factors in the admissions process for the mental patient. First, as Kaplin and Lee (1995) point out, the burden of proving to the court that the alleged mental disability does not inhibit the successful completion of the course of study falls on the plaintiff, not the defendants. It was Doe who had to substantiate to the court that she was otherwise qualified. Second, "...the court considered the fact that she had a recurring illness, even though it was not present at the time of the readmission decision" (Kaplin & Lee, 1995, p. 395). And, it is this second observation of Kaplin and Lee's (1995) that establishes the most consequential implication for the mental patient. It becomes the diagnosis that takes precedence over actual behaviors.

The patient's label is now held in greater scrutiny than his or her actions. For example, referring to the Doe case, in the time between 1977 and 1981, Doe was accepted into a graduate program at Harvard and completed a M.S. degree in the College of Public Health. She was gainfully employed at a professional-level with the Department of Education and Welfare in Washington, D.C. following the completion of her master's degree. During which time, her supervisors rated her performance as "excellent."

Boyle v. Brown University: U.S. District Court (1995)

The defendant—Brown University and various members of the administration—won the case on summary judgment arguing that the alleged events took place prior to the enactment of the Americans with Disabilities Act.

Nonetheless, this case provides valuable practical insight on the administrative authority higher education attempts to exert over those suspected of having psychological problems. This case was brought forth by Ms. Sarah Boyle, a first-year medical student at Brown University College of Medicine. Ms. Boyle claimed that she suffered from chronic fatigue syndrome (CFS) and claimed that the university discriminated against her as a result.

Ms. Boyle had never placed the administration on notice about her alleged CFS disability, but she had independently negotiated with various faculty special testing accommodations. After receiving examination scores that were not to Boyle's satisfaction, she complained to the faculty that the special testing accommodations had not been sufficient. Now, the faculty went to the dean of the college raising questions about Ms. Boyle's psychological fitness. The dean responded—without even having first spoken to the plaintiff—by giving Ms. Boyle one of three options before she would be able to proceed further with her medical studies. First, she could undergo a psychiatric evaluation. Second, she could meet with the Independent Medical Students Committee (IMSC). The IMSC—not a specific committee of the university—was established to provide various forms of support for medical students within the state. Finally, if the plaintiff refused the previous mentioned options, she could face unspecified administrative actions from the university. With reluctance, Ms. Boyle opted to meet with the IMSC.

The IMSC shared with the dean the content of the meetings that took place between Ms. Boyle and the IMSC. Apparently, Ms. Boyle raised some concerns regarding her "behavior" that prompted the dean to formerly respond to Ms. Boyle in a letter stating in part:

> [It would appear] …that you do not have an emotional
> or psychological problem of such duration or severity as
> to affect academic performance… [and] although you
> apparently are able to perform academically, the behav-
> ioral issues remain. These issues must be resolved, par-
> ticularly as you enter the clinical years where your pro-
> fessional behavior with patients, peers and faculty will be
> judged with equal weight as your cognitive knowledge.
> (*Boyle v. Brown University*, 1995, p. 749)

Ms. Boyle also claimed in her action, that the administration
shared with the faculty concerns of her psychological fitness.

Although the case was dismissed, it does raise at
least two interesting points for consideration. First, do institutions of higher education have the right to mandate a student seek mental health treatment or evaluation? At what
point does the institution's concerns for professional development of the student exceed the privacy and right of self-
determination of the student? In the facts presented, the
university's administration considered her academic performance as acceptable. The concern raised is the possibility of
inappropriate behavior/interactions with patients and
peers. Therefore, the university is justified in requesting the
student to seek out psychological intervention. Again, does
this exceed the pedagogical authority of the university? Second, to what extent should knowledge of a student's mental
status be disseminated to faculty? Do faculty have a need to
know this information? What useful purpose does it serve
for faculty to know information that otherwise ought to be
private? Again, there did not appear to be any problem with
Ms. Boyle's academic performance in the classroom. Information that would normally be considered private and con-
fidential should be treated as such by administration and

faculty who become privy to such knowledge from other departments within the university.

## Maczaczyj v. State of New York: U.S. District Court (1997)

Mr. Maczaczyj (plaintiff) sued Empire State College of the State of New York when the college failed to accommodate the plaintiff's disability. The plaintiff was admitted into a master's degree program at the college upon the completion of his undergraduate degree. Although most the graduate program was delivered in a nonresidential format, the program did require 12-credit hours of residency through week long intensive "orientations."

The plaintiff notified the college that he suffered from a host of anxiety disorders such as panic attack disorder, generalized anxiety disorder, and agoraphobia. Thus, he requested from the college an accommodation for his disability. Initially, the plaintiff requested he be excused from participating in the "orientations." The college responded by offering the following accommodation to the plaintiff:

> The plaintiff would (1) be able to be accompanied by a friend or advisor of his choice, (2) have access to a vacant room to which he could retreat whenever the need were to arise, (3) be excused from those portions of the residency which were deemed predominantly of a social nature (i.e., lunch period and coffee break periods), and (4) have his choice of location within the meeting area where the residency is to be conducted. (*Maczaczyj v. State of New York*, 1997, p. 405)

The plaintiff rejected the college's plan for accommodation claiming that any face-to-face interaction was too anxiety provoking. The plaintiff then countered requesting the college to make the orientation available via video conferencing or telephone conference calling. The college denied the request.

In February 1997, the plaintiff sought legal relief from the court. He was claiming that he was being denied reasonable accommodation by Empire State College under Title II of the ADA. "The protections afforded by the ADA ensures that with or without reasonable accommodations of programs and services, a disabled individual who meets the essential eligibility requirements to participate in the program …is not discriminated against by reason of the disability" (*Maczaczyj v. State of New York*, 1997, p. 406).

The college argued to the court that the plaintiff's request for telephonic or two-way video attendance at the required "orientation" would result in pedagogically undermining the academic integrity of the program. Therefore, the proposed accommodation was unreasonable. The court found the defendant's argument the more compelling argument. The court denied the plaintiff's request.

Clearly, this case differs from *Doe v. New York University* in that here the plaintiff's pathology is active. He is currently experiencing his debilitating anxiety. With Doe, however, she was asymptomatic at the time of her claim. The concern with Doe was her propensity for future pathological behavior.

One important implication that potentially derives from this current case, however, is the court's position on technological interventions as a possible "reasonable accommodation." The court took the position of the college that teleconferencing would erode the academic integrity of the curriculum. The concern that arises is whether college administrators may be afforded the opportunity to declare that any technological intervention—like teleconferencing—compromises the pedagogical quality of their program. But, as more classrooms become standardized with this sort of costly technology, the reasonableness of using such technology as an accommodation increases as does the cost of applying it to the home of a single agoraphobic.

Larson v. Snow College: U.S. District Court (2000)

The plaintiff, Ms. Michelle Larson, sued her former college—Snow College—claiming that the college violated her civil rights and discriminated against her in violation of the ADA. In the fall of 1996, Ms. Larson experienced what is vaguely described as "mental health problems" (*Larson v. Snow College*, 2000, p.1290) causing her to seek professional mental health treatment. Upon her return to Snow College two days later, the college administration required that Ms. Larson sign a "Wellness Contract." The contract required, among other criteria, that Ms. Larson be placed on probation of social activities, academic probation and be relieved of her position as Vice-President of the student government. Ms. Larson's complaint alleges that the college employed the use of the Wellness Contract "… as a mechanism to keep her from associating with fellow students and student government officers, to stop her from exercising her free speech rights, and to control her behavior and spy on her while she was in the privacy of her school living quarters" (*Larson v. Snow College*, 2000, p. 1290).

Now, Ms. Larson's compliant has not been resolved by the court. It is ongoing; however, the allegations expressed in the lawsuit provide another level of discussion to the stigmatization the mentally ill face in access to higher education. *Access* does not merely involve admittance to the classroom, but *access* also involves passage to those activities typically associated with the status of student—such as student government involvement and dorm room life. Restricting her access to these activities renders Ms. Larson as a marginal student—a stigmatized student.

Davis v. University of North Carolina: U.S. Court of Appeals (2001)

Ms. Davis sued the University of North Carolina (UNC) following the university's actions to have her removed from a teaching certification program. Ms. Davis was previously diagnosed with dissociative identity disorder (DID). DID refers to a condition were the patient experiences marked changes in personality and memory without any apparent organic explanation (American Psychiatric Association, 2000). In Ms. Davis' case, she experienced occasional blackouts.

It would appear logical based on the facts so far given that UNC was acting within the guidelines of RA and ADA to deny Ms. Davis continued admission in the program. It is necessary for a teacher working with small children not to experience blackouts to ensure the safety of her students. Such a limitation cannot reasonably be accommodated. However, what is alarming about this case is how the appeals courts interpreted Ms. Davis' DID diagnosis. The court argued that RA and ADA did not apply to this case because a psychiatric condition such as DID is too ambiguous to be recognized as a legitimate diagnosis. "Davis has failed to make a prima facie showing that she is disabled within the meaning of the ADA or the Rehabilitation Act ..." (*Davis v. University of North Carolina*, 2001, p. 102).

DID is a recognized by the American Psychiatric Association as a legitimate disorder. It is correct that DID is diagnosed entirely on subjective criteria; however, this is the case with almost all mental illnesses such as depression, mania, schizophrenia, and somatoform disorders. The concern raised here is the court's judgment is determining one disorder legitimate and another illegitimate.

## Analysis and Suggestions for Ameliorating Accessibility for the Mentally Ill: Lessons Being Taught

It appears that institutions of higher education have within the United States employed the use of federal protections, specifically the Rehabilitation Act and the Americans with Disabilities Act, for those dealing with the effects of a mental illness in such a way as to restrict accessibility. Again, it is not my position that institutions of higher education deliberately attempt to restrict assess, seek to discriminate, punish or humiliate the mentally ill. Rather, institutions of higher education serve as reflections of the larger social system. Such actions find deep roots in the values and belief systems within the larger culture. This point may help to explain the various examples of discrimination and inaccessibility discussed in the previous section of this paper, but it does not serve as an excuse for such behavior, nor rationalize its continuation. Institutions of higher education must be concerned with the lessons it teaches to its students through both the formal curriculum within the classroom and the informal curriculum taking the form of administrative policy on the college campus. What then are the lessons being taught to students on college and university campuses?

First, the mentally ill are perceived to be dangerous; higher education administration needs to protect their faculty and students from potentially dangerous people. It can be argued that it was Doe's and Boyle's perceived possibility for violence that may have motivated the administration's policy actions against these students. Was the administration correct in holding such fears? Do the mentally ill have a greater propensity for violence? Are such fears rooted or myth?

Researchers addressing this question would conclude that such fears are seated more in myth than in reality (see Angermeyer, 2000; Link, Phelan, Bresnahan, Stueve, & Pescosolido, 1999; Taylor & Monahan, 1996). Those with mental illness pose no meaningful addition of risk to the physical safety of the general population. Angermeyer even goes as far to say that strangers "...appear to be at an even lower risk of being violently attacked by someone suffering from severe mental disorder than by someone who is mentally healthy" (2000, p. 63). Public perception, however, would suggest otherwise. Perhaps, the public's fear of violence at the hands of the mentally ill is a false projection instituted by the media. As Mulvey and Fardella (2000) argue, the media provides disproportional coverage of isolated acts of violence by the mentally ill creating in the public a misrepresented belief that all mentally ill people must behave similarly. The public has demonstrated a clear absence of comfort with being physically near people known to have a history with mental illness (Link et al., 1999). Unfortunately, it does not appear that these views of the public will ameliorate soon. Rather, "... research suggests that stereotypes of dangerousness are on the increase and that the stigma of mental illness remains a powerfully detrimental feature of the lives of people with such conditions" (Link et al., 1999, p. 1328).

There is a second lesson seen creeping though these profiled court cases. The mentally ill are not capable of functioning in society at an adequate level. Thus, what the mentally ill must contribute to society is little at best. They can't ever function at a level necessary to perform as academics, physicians, lawyers or artists. Certainly, for many of those who experience mental illness, their ability to function is inhibited. But, this is not always the case. History has shown us otherwise. There are countless examples of those with mental illness that have overcome their symptoms, participated and contributed much to the betterment of society.

As a psychotherapist, I have learned as much from my patients on the realities of life and psychological functioning as I ever have from textbooks and lectures. As Kay Redfield Jamison notes when sharing about her own personal experience with bipolar disorder:

> The countless hypomanias, and mania itself, all have brought into my life a different level of sensing and feeling and thinking, Even when I have been most psychotic—delusional, hallucinating, frenzied—I have been aware of finding new corners in my mind and heart... I cannot imagine becoming jaded to life, because I know of those limitless corners, with their limitless views. (1995, p. 218-219)

Suggestions for Policy Reform

In this final section, two suggestions are offered for promoting positive social change. First, higher education administration needs to focus their concerns on behaviors, not diagnosis. A diagnosis is not, in and of itself, a clear predictor for future behavior. One's current and most recent behavior is a better predictor. Asking an admissions candidate about his or her past psychiatric history does not paint as clear of a picture as asking behaviorally relevant questions. In short, any questioning should focus attention on the student's capacity to carry-out his or her academic responsibilities (Alikhan, 2001).

A second substantial way higher education can address the concerns raised in this paper would be to lobby and advocate more strenuously to professional licensure agencies and associations at both the national and state levels. The extent of discrimination faced by the asymptomatic or former mental patients from state bar examiners, for example, is even more severe than those discriminations faced within academia. As Alikhan points out, only seven state bar associations have forgone mental health questioning all together as part of the bar application process, but 32 states still engage in a wide range of inquiry as to an applicant's mental health history (2001). Applicants could face discriminatory questions such as "Have you, within the past five years, been treated or counseled for a mental, emotional or nervous disorder" (Alikhan, 2001, p. 159). As Reske explains, one of basic assumptions for employing broad questioning to bar applicants has been the belief that having sought treatment for a mental condition poses a greater danger to the public's safety both physically and professionally (1995). "[T]he bar is feeding stereotypes which pervade society, including an attitude that those who seek psychological counseling are deviant, weak, or prone to error" (Alikhan, 2001, p. 163).

Such a rationale is misguided on several accounts. First, as previously stated, the mentally ill—even those actively experiencing psychosis—pose no significant risk to the safety of the rest of us. Second, such broad inquiry may fail to take into consideration the extensive range of mental conditions that are legitimately recognized by the American Psychiatric Association (APiA). The extent of possible mental illness that one could be diagnosed with is perhaps broader than the degree of questioning by state bar examiners. For instance, the APiA's primary classification system used to diagnosis psychopathology—*The Diagnostic and Statistical Manual of Mental Disorders: Fourth Edition—Text Revision*—includes the following diagnostic labels: nicotine dependence, parent-child relational problem, and caffeine dependence (2000). For example, if one has been prescribed Zyban by their physician to help them stop smoking, one has technically been treated for a recognized psychiatric condition. Finally, this rationale discourages people from seeking help. "Mental health inquires might keep people from seeking counseling or treatment, or cause those in treatment to be 'less than totally candid with their therapist' for fear of disclosure" (Reske, 1995, p. 24).

At some level, we are all different and face the possibility of discrimination and unfair treatment based on our differences whether they be the color of our skin, gender, religion, disability or place of national origin. For the mentally ill, however, such discrimination appears to be more inherent within the subtleness of daily social life. Discrimination for the mentally ill is not a discrete event.

It is vital to point out that, despite its ideals, institutions of higher education also play a role in the continuation of stigma and discrimination of the mentally ill on college and university campuses. Such actions are not intentional, but nonetheless they are present, and lives are impacted thus. If the goal of education is to assist in fostering independence, compassion, creativity, and excellence in students, it is vital for higher education to be fully aware of its own limitations and strive for excellence in seeking resolution.

# 10 Psycholiterature: The Psychology of Literature

The idea to twirl together psychology and literature is not new. Psychologists have made some share of contributions to the body of fictional literature (e.g., Elaine Hatfied's *Rosie*, David Liebert's *Unreasonable Sanity*, M. Scott Peck's *A Bed by the Window*, and Noam Shpancer's *The Good Psychologist*). Moreover, those in the practice of clinical psychology/psychoanalysis have drawn on the talents of fictional writers in an effort to facilitate treatment. Psychoanalyst Alma Bond (2002) notes, when reading outside of the clinician's office we may find ourselves getting lost in stories, but when stories are prescribed in context of treatment, they may help us to find ourselves too. Yet, literature can also be used to facilitate the process of teaching and learning in psychology classrooms as well.

Combining the use of literature with the study of psychology, henceforth referred to as *psycholiterature,* refers to an active, reciprocal experience of applying literature to engage a deeper understanding, appreciation and awareness for both the study of psychology, as well as the study of literature. It is an applied methodological strategy to both aid and engage the student in the pursuit of *knowing* psychology through the study of fiction literature.

## On Science

Authors of introductory psychology textbooks routinely open their dialogue with students by defining psychology as *a scientific study of behavior and mental activity* where the word *science* has come to stand almost exclusively to mean an *empirical* science where absolute knowledge is both observable and void of ambiguity. Imbedded in psycholiterature is an assumption that a *scientific study of behavior and mental activity* can also embrace ambiguity; a methodology does not have to exclusively employ quantitative means of analysis in order to observe some inherent truth about psychology. Quantitative empiricism has its limitations; moreover, there is no shortage of examples—both classic and contemporary—pointing to this fact.

Consider Stanley Milgram's (1963) descriptive study on the *Obedience to Authority;* his initial findings suggested nearly two-thirds of subjects tested would follow the matter-of-fact requests made by the experimenter, "The experiment requires that you continue... You must go on" (p. 375). Even six years following countless replications and the publication of Migram's (1969) book, in the final analysis all he was ever able to show was roughly two-thirds of his subjects when prompted would deliver a mortal level of electric current to a stranger. We all begin the discussion of *Obedience to Authority* saying to ourselves, *I wouldn't do such a thing to a stranger.* But, we end the discussion now questioning ourselves, *Could I do such a thing to a stranger?* Milgram was never able to offer solace to this question. He leaves us in a state of existential terror. His suggestions explaining possible predictive factors differentiating those who find themselves in the one-third minority versus those falling into the two-thirds majority was simply speculative. This is the inherent limitation of descriptive research; it merely defines the research population. Such a study lacks depth and prediction.

Does Milgram tell us anything more certain and true about the nature of human conformity than what we might, otherwise, learn from Shirley Jackson's (1948) "The Lottery?" Similarly, Milgram's subjects parade voluntarily down the dark basement corridor of Yale's psychology laboratory at a pace no different than Jackson's villagers do on that bright sunny, June morning. In each instance, the reader—whether it be of *science* or *literature*—must confront the horror of what is to follow haven now confronted the *box*. Jackson offers psychology students a different context to examine for what is a common question for both she and Milgram.

This discussion is not suggesting scientific inquire is flawed, yielding no product of value. There is great value to be had though scientific pursuit! Our lives have been enriched tremendously due to science. Rather, the point being made here is simple: empirical science is limited. Coming to know something through objective means is not inherently superior to knowledge obtained through subjective means. Moreover, literature offers the student of psychology a subjective pathway for knowing something.

## On Feelings

Perhaps Rene Descartes' is most remembered for his proclamation, "I think; therefore, I am." But, he could have just as well uttered, "I feel; therefore, I am conscious." Feelings by their nature refer to a self-awareness of our personal emotions (Damasio, 1999). As Frosh (2011) points out, the act of experiencing a feeling is the very recognition of one's existence. There is no consciousness that is not self-consciousness. Thus, psychologists are inherently interested in the subject of feelings. Yet, as many young men struggling with writing a love letter can attest, feelings can often be evasive and brutish to capture accurately with words.

One's verbal intelligence is not positively correlated with one's range, depth or capacity to be emotionally self-aware. In this sense, words merely provide a means by which we hitch our feelings to a linguistic, cognitive context.

Incorporating the use of literature to facilitate self-awareness, encourages us to, not only be aware of feelings present within our consciousness, although difficult to articulate, but to actually engage in deeper self-awareness by acknowledging, perhaps for the first time, feelings we are not even aware we are, in fact, feeling. As Frosh explains, "people can only allow themselves to feel things only when they are safe enough to face the consequences" (2011, p. 66) of their feelings. In such instances, literature can offer safe harbor by allowing our feelings to be projected on to literature. Consider for a moment, Maurice Sendak's (1963) classic children's story, *Where the Wild Things Are.* The story of Max and his mystical journey to the island where the Wild Things live has been read to children, grandchildren and now great grandchildren since first published in 1963. In these simple ten sentences, we find a story on how children deal with their feelings of anger at parents, or in this case a mother. We connect with the story; it resonates with us across the generations because we can identify with Max's emotional plight.

Feelings also serve as a form of social adhesive connecting us to other people. "Feelings are social: they pass through people, infecting each other" (Frosh, 2011, p. 13). Sharing one's feeling is an act of intimacy. "How are you doing?" may be the most human question we can ask another person. Literature is a means by which we mutually tether our feelings to in company with others. With literature, we can share a common emotional experience. Thus, it might be argued, stories are a fundamental building block for any civilization.

On Theory

Literature provides a means for the exploration into the depth and application of psychological theory. Theoretical concepts can be analyzed and manipulated in ways nonfictional writing simply cannot lend itself to provide. The pioneering German sociologist, Max Weber (1949) argued in an effort to make valid and precise observations of our social world the social scientist is wise to employ the use of *ideal types* referring to a hypothetical construct based on extracting just the pure characteristics of the phenomenon being studied, in this instance, psychological theory. Literature may serve as an ideal type for exploring, comparing, contrasting, classifying, and measuring psychological theory. Consider William Golding's (1954) *Lord of the Flies*, the allegorical story not only serves as a demonstration of conscious-unconscious interaction with the reader, but directly addresses Sigmund Freud's (1990) theoretical discussion on Thanatos, showing how our inherent death instinct will inevitably serve as our downfall. "Maybe there is a beast... maybe it's only us" (Golding, 1954, p. 80).

Additionally, literature can serve as the basis for which psychological theory is drawn and refined. Again, case in point, Sigmund Freud's psychodynamic ideas on gender acquisition and fixation during the phallic stage of development were significantly influenced by literature. "The myth of King Oedipus, who killed his father and took his mother to wife, reveals, with little modification, the infantile wish, which is later opposed and repudiated by the barrier against incest, Shakespeare's *Hamlet* is equally rooted in the soil of the incest-complex, but under a better disguise" (Freud, 1961, p. 51).

For purpose of effective acquisition, understanding and learning of new psychological theory, literature may serve as an efficient and precise pedagogical tool promoting a deep, holistic appreciation of the concept for the student. The use of literature to this end helps students to appreciate the actual application and analysis of psychological theory over mere definitional knowledge and understanding. Consider the use of A. S. Byatt's (2005) "The Thing in the Forest" as a tool for teaching students Carl Jung's idea of a *collective unconscious*. Perhaps, this just might be a story about murder where the loathly worm severs as an archetype for the story's two main characters, Penny and Primrose.

In conclusion, the use of literature can serve as a useful pedagogical tool for facilitating the teaching and learning of psychology in the classroom. Additionally, adopting a psycholiterature perspective creates opportunities for cross discipline collaboration, possibilities for co-teaching and writing across the curriculum. In so doing, students are asked to think and consider ideas deeply and critically. We make the curriculum more meaningful and relevant, thereby, preparing our students to compete in an ever increasingly complex and competitive world.

# 11 "For it is just this question of pain that parts us."[14] [15]

> *In a world full of danger, to be a potentially seeable object is to be constantly exposed to danger. Self-consciousness, then, maybe the apprehensive awareness of oneself as potentially exposed to danger by the simple fact of being visible to others. The obvious defense against such a danger is to make oneself invisible in one way or another.* –R. D. Laing, M.D. [16]

It was an odd summer. No longer between semesters, rather between degrees, Jerry moved back into his bedroom. This was once his home, now smaller and older. He once shared the room with his brother, Stephen, who was three years older, recently married, a school teacher, now living outside of Atlanta. Jerry was no longer a college student and not yet a law school student. He returned the night before last with a duffle bag of clothes (mostly t-shirts and jeans) and a newly minted degree in British Literature. Jerry hadn't unpacked the duffle yet, avoiding the feeling of permanent

---

[14] Well, H. G. (1896). *The island of Dr. Moreau.* United Kingdom: Heinemann, Stone & Kimball.

[15] This short story was originally published in a collection of short stories by the author: Liebert, D. (2014). *Shrink wrapped: Stories from a psychologist's unconscious.* Abbeville, SC: Moonshine Cove Publishing.

[16] Laing, R. D. (1965). *The divided self: An existential study in sanity and madness.* New York: Penguin.

residency. He preferred to see himself as a guest, drifting for the next three months before moving on to Vanderbilt. He didn't completely belong here anymore.

Neither, Mike nor Trisha, had any empty nest reaction when Jerry, their youngest, moved out of state for school. In fact, they embraced the change, falling comfortably back into their role once upon a time as a devout married couple, no longer a family of four. There was less rushing, more wine, comfort with their careers, and better sex. Nonetheless, they were both glad to see their son back home for the summer. They welcomed him and congratulated him once again on finishing his BA with *cum laude* distinction.

Jerry was no bother. He mostly spent his time up alone in his room reading. Long, skinny legs would carry him daily down to the library. He could spend hours every morning wandering the shelves followed by more hours back up in his room devouring his finds.

Jerry would come down from his room now and again throughout the day to pick. He ate like a bird, opening the refrigerator, picking at cold food. It had always been like this, eating only cold food. Mike and Trisha still had their dinners in the dining room, cloth napkins laid out, with the table set for two. Trisha would leave a plate in the refrigerator for Jerry to pick at later.

Jerry's weight had been a constant source of conflict. There were arguments over it when he was a child refusing to eat. Trisha took Jerry once to Dr. Spencer, their family physician, who suggested vitamins and more patience on Trisha's part. "He'll outgrow it," Spencer reassured her. Jerry took his vitamins; Trisha stopped outright arguing with Jerry over food favoring a more passive approach. On Tuesday Trisha asked Jerry if there was anything in particular he wanted her to pick up from the supermarket on her way home from work.

"Coffee is okay, but I would also like some radishes and scallops."

"...Coffee, radishes, and scallops?"

"Yes, I want round food."

"Round?" Trisha asked with a smile.

"I believe our bodies better absorb round food. I need to start eating more round foods," Jerry responded without acknowledging Trisha's smile.

Trisha interpreted the dialog as her son's odd way of asking her to back-off, stop bothering him about his dietary habits. Trisha did not press, nor did she buy radishes and scallops later that day.

Before the sun broke through the following day, Mike got out of bed. The cat was scratching at their bedroom door determined to get in and up on the bed. The bedroom was dark. Mike opened the door noticing light seeping out underneath Jerry's closed door. Mike opened his door wider. He listened. Mumbling. He could hear Jerry mumbling something but couldn't make out the words. Was he on the phone? Could there be a girlfriend? Singing along to a song masked by headphones? Mike cracked his door just in case the cat changed his mind, then he returned back to bed.

Later in the morning, before noon, Trisha called Mike at the office. "You have to get down to the library. It's Jerry. Something's wrong! They'll call the police if one of us doesn't get down there right away." Mike's office was much closer to the library. He hurried.

A police car followed Mike into the library's parking lot. A mother dropping off her daughter for Summer Book Camp overheard the commotion, taking matters into her own hands, and called the police herself. The police cruiser parked right out front in the fire lane. Jerry had to park in the back, but he jogged from his car to the lobby where he saw the officer now talking to one of the librarians standing at the front desk. She pointed at Mike. "That's his father."

Mike didn't stop. He could hear Jerry on the far side of the library yelling. Jerry was backed up to wall-length, ceiling to floor window overlooking a pond. Not moving from his position, Jerry was shifting his weight from his right leg to the left, moving back and forth. He was holding both his hands out, fingers spread wide as if about to be attacked by a rabid dog. "Nobody is listening to me. Why won't anybody listen to me!" Jerry yelled.

"I'm listening," Mike said. "Tell me what's going on?"

"They're changing all the words! The words are being changed!"

"What words?" Mike asked. He kept his eye fixed on his son but could feel that someone, the police officer perhaps, had walked up behind him.

Now with both his hands, Jerry pointed towards the librarians at the reservation desk, "They are back there changing all the words in the books. That's what they've been doing all this time." Jerry was no longer yelling, rather, his words came out in a desperate cry. Mike saw agony in Jerry's face. Torture. "They're changing all the words." Jerry was now pointing at open books sitting on the table a few feet away from him. "'What a piece of work is man! How noble in reason! How infinite in faculty! In form and moving how express and admirable! In action how like an angel! In apprehension how like a god! The beauty of the world, the paragon of animals!' This is what it is supposed to say in Hamlet. But, they have changed it. See!"

"Is there a problem with drugs?" a voice said behind Mike's ear.

"No." Mike whispered back.

"Mental illness?"

"No," again said in a soft whisper.

"You need to get him to agree to go to the hospital with you, or I'll need to take him into custody."

"Jerry, we'll get to the bottom of this. I promise. Together you and I will figure this all out. But, you have to listen to me. Can you do that?" Mike struggled to make his voice calm and soft.

"But, they are changing...."

"If you come with me right now, we will figure this out. We can't figure this out here. We have to leave. Will you come with me?" Mike asked while holding his hand out to his son.

Jerry took his father's hand and the two began to walk through the library together. The children from Summer Book Camp watched from their seated position on the blue rug, sitting Indian style, they were no longer interested in Dr. Seuss. As they neared the exit, Jerry paused and began again to rant. "But, those cock suckers are back there changing all the words! I've discovered...."

"Jerry, we have to keep walking. I need for you to calmly tell me everything that you have learned. You have to tell me calmly, so I can better understand, what you have learned. Tell me everything."

They started walking again. Jerry started to explain, calmer now, how he first noticed H. G. Well's *The Island of Dr. Moreau* was being changed, morphed, from the original. The story was no longer told from the character Edward Prendick's point of view. Now Dr. Moreau was narrating the entire story. Facts had been changed. Mike did not interrupt, allowing Jerry to elaborate the entire ride to the hospital. The police car slowly followed behind.

Mike drove around to the back of the hospital where the Emergency Room was located. Both a man and a woman waited outside the ER bay doors where the ambulances would arrive. When seeing Mike's car, they began to wave to pull up straight to the bay. The police officer must have called ahead.

"Why are we here?" Jerry asked.

"We will get to the bottom of this. I promised you. Now, I need for you to trust me."

Mike and Jerry were greeted with kind smiles and softly spoken words.

"I'll take your keys and park the car for you," an orderly said wearing green scrubs. "I'm Lynda. Please, follow me," the woman requested.

They followed her to an examination room. Green curtains were drawn closed. For the first time, Jerry was quiet, although quivering. Within just a couple of minutes, the curtain was opened.

"Good morning, I'm Dr. Montgomery, the on-call psychiatrist. What seems to be the problem?"

Jerry's eyes widened. Adrenaline pulsed. He had taken a seat on the examination table, but now fell backwards catching himself with his left hand. He took a deep breath, face turning red, he held it in. Turning first to see if his father was still in the room, Jerry redirected his attention back at the doctor and with his exhale of wind words came shrieking out. "You're Dr. Moreau! You're going to vivisect[17] me!" Turning back towards his father screaming, "Don't let him cut me! Don't let him cut me!"

"I'm not Moreau. I'm Dr. Montgomery. There is no Dr. Moreau who works here at the hospital."

Mike said, "He's not Moreau. I promise you. Please trust me. He's not Moreau. Jerry fell silent, now holding his terror close to his chest.

---

[17] A surgery done on a live organism for experimental purposes.

"Jerry, what if my nurse, Lynda, stayed with you for just a few minutes while your father and I spoke outside. Would that be okay?"

The two men took Jerry's silence to mean acceptance. Lynda came into the examination room as the father and psychiatrist stepped out.

"Your son is experiencing a paranoid psychotic episode. Has anything like this happened before?

"No."

"Is he using drugs?"

"I'm almost certain he's never tried drugs, not even alcohol."

"How old is your son?" The doctor now asked.

"Twenty-one. He'll be Twenty-two in October."

"I'm going to suggest an injection of Haloperidol. If he is agreeable. That'll help and help quickly. Afterwards, we'll talk to see what the next step should be."

"Okay."

The two men returned back to the examination room. Lynda continued to stay as well. "Jerry, I believe you are sick; you have psychosis and need some medication. Do I have your permission to give you some medication, an anti-psychotic?"

"No! No! I don't want you to change me into some form of beast! You can't cut me open and look inside! I'm not going to be part of your experiment! I want off this fucking island!"

"It's just medication," Dr. Montgomery said.

"No. I won't let you cut open my mind, look inside, vivisect me!"

"Okay, okay," Montgomery said motioning to Mike to step outside the examination room again to speak.

"In the eyes of the law, Jerry is an adult. As long as he isn't showing signs of suicide or homicide risk, he has the right to refuse treatment. There is nothing I can do for him at the moment. There are professional ethics to be considered here. "

"But doctor, he thinks you're a character from a novel."

***

Mike and Jerry returned back to the house. Trisha left work early and was anxiously waiting the return of her two men. Upon seeing Jerry, Trisha's eyebrows immediately arched as her mouth turned down and opened some. Anguish. It wasn't so much his physical appearance as his affect. Jerry looked disheveled right from the core. Eyes darting to and fro, Jerry looked lost in his own living room. Jerry wasn't Jerry anymore, turning into an altogether different species.

"Oh, my God!"

"Trisha, for Jerry's sake everything is going to be fine."

"I need to go to my room. I need to check my books, make sure nothing has been changed. The words are still the way they all wrote them." Jerry again began to shift his weight from right leg to left.

"Okay. We'll check in on you shortly."

"The bastard did nothing? Nothing?" Trisha said only once Jerry had left the room.

"Something about professional ethics? He doesn't have the capacity to be unsupervised in a public library, but he can make an informed medical decision? Can you believe that bullshit! .... What are we going to do? He's really sick!"

"I called Dr. Spencer's office. He's at a conference today, but said he'll see Jerry first thing tomorrow morning. He'll practice medicine, not social philosophy."

"What do we do until then?"

"Valium. I'll give him one of my Valium; at least, it will help him sleep."

Trisha knocked on Jerry's door as she opened it with Mike following behind her. Jerry was crouched on the floor like a cat, toes, knees, and elbows on the floor, lurching over a book frantically searching words. "Honey, I want you to take this medicine for me." Trisha held out her hand with the pill center in her palm."

"No."

"But, its round. Round medicine is good for you."

Jerry paused looking at his mother. Thinking. "Okay." Jerry stood up, took the medicine with the water Mike had brought up with him, then returned back to his cat-like stance peering over the book left open on the floor.

"Honey, would it be all right if I just sat here with you? I promise not to disturbed you."

"Can I let you know if I find any changes to the words, okay?"

"Sure, Honey." Trisha turned over to Mike." Let the two of us be alone for a while."

Mike gave a quick nod and left the room. Trisha sat on the corner of her son's bed watching him run his finger over every line of text. First his fingers ran from left to right followed by right to left for the next line of text working his way down each page. She examined the room. His duffel bag was sitting on the floor next to the closet unpacked. His bookshelf was all but empty. On the wall under the window, books were stacked like one of the Great Pyramids of Egypt. A card had been positioned on the windowsill just above the literary pyramid. On the front of the card, Trisha could make out a picture of a graduation cap tossed in the air. She continued to watch her son for the hour it took the Valium to nestle into Jerry's system and sleep to take over. Now asleep on the floor, Trisha walked to the window, picking up the card, began to read. "Congratulations to my baby brother. I'm so proud of you! First a degree on learning to read stories. Next a degree on how to change them. My brother, the law student! Love Stephen."

Trisha returned the card back on the windowsill, re-turned to her son's bed to lie down. She watched him sleep then joined him. Waking up two hours later, Trisha looked around the room. "Where's Jerry?"

***

The voices were too loud to keep Jerry asleep for long. In fact, the voices had been keeping him awake for days now. No sleep whatsoever. They would overlap, talking one on top of the other. Their words were confusing, offering no clear sense of direction. Jerry awoke with a clearer sense of what needed to be done now. Finally, the voices were making sense. Perhaps the medicine his mother had given him earlier was working after all. Round medicine works. Jerry quietly left his room not wanting to disturb his mother. He made his way down stairs to find his father asleep in the living room. The local news had just started on the television. Jerry left through the back door off the kitchen.

Jerry had only known H. G. Wells, Shakespeare, and Tennyson through their words, the stories and poems he had read. Now he could hear them. He could actually hear them, and they were all speaking to him more clearly than they ever had before. Jerry had been commissioned, an of-ficer of the highest rank, of the Light Brigade. He had been given his orders. The battle was soon to be afoot. Jerry was off to Balaclava.

His comrades had been captured, taken as prisoners of war. Under military orders, Jerry was charged with freeing them. He knew the layout of the prison camp better than anyone else. This, no doubt, was the reason he was chosen to lead the mission. He would breach the enemy's camp, proceed immediately to their cell, extract, make way back to central command, and fortify. No doubt the enemy will launch a counter attack in retaliation. Jerry needed to make himself ready.

He soon arrived on the outskirts of Balaclava. The camp was in clear view. The gates had been left without any sentry. It was now or never. Jerry launched his offensive, running with cat-like agility at full speed through the gates, directly to the prison cell. Jerry quickly scanned the collection of inmates trying to locate his comrades amongst the herd. "Found you!" Jerry shouted. "And, you!" With Tennyson, Wells, and Shakespeare in hand, once again on the run, Jerry made his retreat. A sentry had now been dispatched at the gate. He gave a push before the enemy had time to ready her sword. Down she went hitting the ground hard.

Jerry never stopped running. Within a minute, he could hear the enemy's sirens. They were about to launch their counter offensive. He had to retreat back to the fort as soon as possible in order to stand a fighting chance. Winded and physically spent, Jerry slowly approached the fort, their central command. He looked closely; it had been abandoned. Everyone's gone. Had there been an attack? Why the retreat? Still under orders, Jerry had to find his own way into the locked fortress. He had his comrades wait while he found a rock of suitable size. The glass window crumbled and Jerry, along with his comrades, were soon safely inside their fortress.

The rooms of the fortress were dark. Jerry turned on the lights. Make no mistake about it; he was ready for the enemy. He was ready for war. When they arrived to, which he knew would be at any moment, he wanted them to know just where to find him. Within ten minutes, three enemy vehicles had approached. He could spot soldiers on the move. He could hear them running down the hallway. How did they breach the fortress so quickly? Just who is this enemy? They were in the room swarming.

"Put your hands up! Don't move!"

"Run Wells! Get out of here Tennyson!"

Jerry felt the enemy take hold of his body first at the back of the neck, then his right arm. Forced to the floor, his arms were restrained with shackles.

"I'm not going back to Balaclava!" Jerry screamed.

\*\*\*

Mike and Trisha searched the house only to find the back door ajar.

"He's gone!"

"Where would he go?"

"Maybe the library?"

As they turned the corner, merging into the entry lane to the library, they saw flashing lights. Two police cars and an ambulance. Neither spoke a word, worried doing so would push the other over the brink into a nightmare. Until they were told otherwise, their son was safe and unharmed. Neither wanted to ruin that hope for the other.

"What happened?" Mike asked the first police officer he saw, who was just a boy no older than Jerry.

\*\*\*

Jerry was in a room all to himself, a hospital room. At first he thought it was a dungeon, a makeshift military prison, believing this because his mind told him this was so. Now his mind was telling him he was in a hospital. His thoughts and perceptions were changing.

For weeks, his thoughts had been disturbing him. He might be reading and all of a sudden the book was saying something back. The author telling him something special, unknown to anyone else who had ever read their stories. He felt like a young teenager being tempted, coerced by would-be buddies to participate in mischief, reluctant, still knowing right from wrong, but desperately wanting to fit in, to be part of the in-crowd. Jerry decided to give into his mind's temptation, a form of neuro peer pressure, and ignore all the other voices, like his parents, professors, and his few

friends left back at college. Jerry simply became a ghost, sur-
rendering his will to the cognitive machine within.

Giving in to his mind's suggestion felt comfortable, wel-
coming as an old friend. Until that moment, it was as if he
had been swimming against the current of a fast-moving
river. Now he was simply letting his mind go limp, the current taking over. Unlike before, it all made sense. There was
purpose, clarity, and direction as the current picked up
speed, churning white water.

It was only an hour ago, the prison guard from the enemy force, injected him with poison, probably a truth serum
in order to make him divulge military secrets. He tried to
resist, but his arms were shackled. Jerry closed his eyes con-
tinuing to imagine he was being carried through the white
waters of his mind. Within minutes, the rushing water began
to subside; it was no longer so deep, quickly becoming shal-
low. He hit a rock underneath, followed by another one.
Now there was a different force, a new force dragging him
to shore, wringing out the pathologically saturated pores of
his mind. Jerry's psychosis was fading away; a state of sobri-
ety once again restored.

As the medication achieved a state of sanity, clarity, Jerry
was reminded of his actions throughout the day: The scene
in the library that morning, his father taking him to the hospital, the pyramid of books, pushing the librarian, Ms. Rose,
to the ground, and the final incident occurring at the high
school where it all came to an end and the police took him
into custody and had him involuntarily hospitalized.

Ms. Rose was always so kind. She encouraged Jerry to
pursue a major in literature. He'd know her since he was a
child. She read Sendack's *Where the Wild Things Are* to him
on Saturday mornings. His memory was unleashing images
of him pushing her to the ground. She wasn't an enemy

combatant; she was his friend. Did his actions result in any injury to her? He truly hoped not.

Jerry felt a wave of shame crashing over him. He wanted to hide, disappear, and fade away into nothing. At that moment, Jerry wished he could jump back into the white foamy waters of his psychosis. Life would truly be easier to face if psychotic. The antipsychotic drug had vivisected his psyche, opening the inner workings of his cognitive machine for self-examination. The horror of his psychosis was thrust upon him as he lay restrained in his hospital bed.

# 12 That'll be $200K

The two graduate degrees typically earned and necessary for the practice of clinical psychology are the Ph.D. (Doctor of Philosophy) and the Psy.D. (Doctor of Psychology). A typical question undergraduate students ask in an abnormal psychology class when discussing education requirements to practice as a psychologist centers around the difference between these two degrees: is one more marketable, easier to earn or qualifies the practitioner to do more with patents. The actual differences are minimal; Psy.D. programs are more structured and focus more on clinical practice; whereas, Ph.D. programs place more emphasis on research. But, these differences are overall minimal. Thus, my reply gets right to the point: The only real difference between the two degrees is about $125,000. Graduate school is expensive. The average amount of debt for students completing a Ph.D. is about $75,000, whereas Psy.D. students' average rate of debt was about $200,000 (Stinger, 2016). Thus, the only real difference between the two degrees is their cost. This is because most Ph.D.'s tend to be earned at state universities where students benefit from in-state tuition rates, and Psy.D.'s are earned at private colleges/universities. Moreover, most graduate programs—Ph.D. or Psy.D,—in clinical psychology offer students little to no opportunities for scholarships or other sources of funding to cover their expenses. Students pay tuition and other fees out of their own pockets, meaning most students borrow through federally funded student loans programs the cost for their graduate training. Regardless, where one earns his or her degree, professional training in clinical psychology is expensive. Unfortunately, all too often this piece of information isn't discussed in undergraduate psychology classes. "The cost of education and the impact of student debt, particularly as debt is emerging as a new sociological category of poverty in the United States" (Doran, Marks, Kraha, Ameen & El-Ghoroury, 2016, p. 9).

This is a reality to becoming a clinical psychologist today; those new to the professional practice of clinical psychology are saddled with a lot of student debt today. A typical monthly student loan payment, based on 4% annual interest rate with a 30-year repayment plan would be about $950.00 per month. This means for the student who completes all their graduate work at the age of 28, he or she will be making a monthly payment of $950 until reaching the age of 58, at which time the total amount paid over the lifetime of the loan will have been $342,000. Despite such high figures, most students who are currently pursuing their graduate work as well as those who have recently graduated still say, if given the option to choose a different career path, they would still would pursue clinical psychology (Winerman, 2016).

Although these numbers sound high, the cost of obtaining such professional training is relative. It's relative in that it can only be understood when psychologists' typical incomes are discussed alongside average tuition costs. It's important to know just how much psychologists typically earn. According a report conducted by the National Science Foundation (2013), the median annual salary for psychologists was $80,000 with 57% of all psychologists earning an annual salary within the range of $60,000 to $120,000. This same report shows that psychologists who work in private practice earned about $97,000 annual, which is more than those who work in either the government sector or in teaching positions. Those psychologists, however, who worked in management-level positions supervising other clinicians earned the highest salaries, as much as $155,000 a year. Another study suggests salaries can range greatly based on the specialty of the psychologist, which ranges widely. Those specializing in working with children averaged $150,000 annually, neuropsychologists earned $155,000, and forensic psychologists seem to be earning some of the highest annual salaries with reported median incomes at $215,000 per year (Doran et al., 2016).

The above data is vitally important to undergraduate students considering future careers in clinical psychology for several reasons. First, one should have clear and fair expectations on what their economic life will be like once established in a new career. Second, the prime time to make rational choices—or reasonable tradeoffs—as to specific areas of practice begins while still in undergraduate school. For instance, students might want to consider working with specific patient populations that pay better. For example, marriage counseling tends to pay better than gerontology-related work. Neuropsychology pays better than being an assistant professor of psychology at the local community college. Some areas of specialization are more difficult to transition into once established in practice; it's just easier to initially train towards the specialty while still in school.

Undergraduate as well as graduate students may also want to consider strategies for managing the volume of student loan debt they will be assuming as well as creative ways to pay it off quickly. Newly established programs offered by student loan servers allow the graduate to make lower monthly payments if initial salaries are low. Also, consider for instance, many clinical psychologists report rewarding careers working as military psychologists where

they go into the military with officer-level rank. As one of
the benefits, the military will pay on student loan debt.
There are also other government sponsored programs
where newly graduated psychologists work in underserved
areas and, by agreeing to do so for a specified period, the
government pays on the student loan. It is also important to
be making wise decisions while in undergraduate school.
The goal should be to come out of undergraduate school
with the least amount of student loan debt as possible.
Don't borrow more than what is needed to cover tuition
and other direct educational expenses. Complete the first
two years at the local community college. Although living
on campus might seem like a welcomed idea, try to choose
a university that is geographically closer to home in the
hopes parents will continue to cover living expenses and do
laundry.

Finally, don't forget your great-aunt's birthday who
is now well into her 90s living alone with 12 cats.

# References

Alexander, J. (2012). *The hidden psychology of pain: The use of understanding to heal chronic pain.* Bloomington, IL: Balboa Press.

Alikhan, M. (2001). The ADA is narrowing mental health inquires on bar applications: Looking to the medical profession to decide where to go from here. *Georgetown Journal of Legal Ethics, 14,* 159-177.

American Psychiatric Association. (2000). *The diagnostic and statistical manual of mental disorders: Fourth edition—text revision.* Washington, DC: Author.

American Psychiatric Association. (2013). *Diagnostic and statistical manual of mental disorders (5th ed.).* Arlington, VA: American Psychiatric Publishing.

American Psychiatric Association. (2013b). Changing the practice and perception of psychiatry: 2013 annual report. Arlington, VA: American Psychiatric Association.

American Psychological Association. (n.d.). APA membership statistics. Author. Retrieved from http://apa.org/about/apa/achieves/membership.aspx

Angel, M. (1996). *Science of trail: The clash of medical evidence and the law in the breast implant case.* New York: Norton.

Angermeyer, M. C. (2000). Schizophrenia and violence. *Acta Psychiatrica, 102,* 63-67.

*Boyle v. Brown University*, 881 F. Supp. 747 (D. Rhode Island 1995).

Blom, J. D. (2010). *A dictionary of hallucinations.* New York: Springer.

Bond, A. H. (2002). *Tales of psychology: Short stories to make you wise.* St. Paul, MI: Paragon House.

Byatt, A. S. (2005). *Little black book of stories.* New York: Vintage.

Caballero, J. & Nahata, M. C. (2005). Selective serotonin reuptake inhibitors and suicidal ideation and behavior in children. *American Journal of Health-System Pharmacy, 62 (8),* 864-868.

Carroll, L. (1984). *Alice's adventures in wonderland & through the looking-glass.* New York: Bantam Classics.

Chang, K. (2007). Adult bipolar disorder is continuous with pediatric bipolar disorder. *The Canadian Journal of Psychiatry, 52 (7),* 418-424.

Cooper, D. (1967). *Psychiatry and anti-psychiatry.* United Kingdom: Paladin.

Comer, R. J. (2002). *Fundamentals of abnormal psychology (3rd ed.).* New York: Worth.

Damasio, A. (1999). *The feeling of what happens: Body and emotion in the making of consciousness.* New York: Hardcort Brace.

*Davis v. University of North Carolina,* 263 F.3d 95. (U.S. 4 Circuit 2001).

*Doe v. New York University,* 666 F.2d 761, (U.S. 2 Circuit 1981).

Doran, J. M., Marks, L. R., Kraha, A., Ameen, E. J., & El-Ghoroury N. H. (2016). Graduate debt in psychology: A qualitative analysis. *Training and Education in Professional Psychology, 10,* 3-13.

Dos Reis, S., Zito, J. M., Safter, D. J., & Soeken, K. L. (2001). Mental health services for youth in foster care and disabled youth. *American Journal of Public Health, 91,* 1094-1099.

Fontanella, C. A., Hiance, D. L., Phillips, G. S., et al. (2014). Trends in psychotrophic medication use for Medicaid-enrolled preschool children. *Journal of Child and Family Studies, 23,* 617-631.

Freud, S. (1990). *Beyond the pleasure principle.* New York: W.W. Norton.

Freud, S. (1961). *Five lectures on psycho-analysis.* New York: W.W. Norton.

Frosh, S. (2011). *Feelings.* New York: Routledge.

Goffman, E. (1959). *Asylums: Essays on the social situation of mental patients and other inmates.* New York: Anchor Books.

Golding, W. (1954). *Lord of the flies.* Boston: Faber & Faber.

Grahek, N. (2007). *Feeling pain and being in pain (2nd ed.).* Cambridge, MA: The MIT Press.

Horwitz, A. V. & Wakefield, J. C. (2007). *The loss of sadness: How psychiatry transformed normal sorrow into depressive disorder.* New York: Oxford University Press.

Insel, T. (2011). Director's blog: Mental illness defined as disruption in neural circuits. National Institute of Mental Health. Retrieved from http://www. Nimh.gov/about/director/2011/mental-illness-defined-as-dirsruption-in- nural-circits.shtml

Jackson, S. (1948). The lottery. *The New Yorker, June 26, 24-28.*

Jacoby, R. (1975). *Social amnesia: A critique of conformist psychology from Adler to Laing.* New York: Beacon.

Jamison, K. R. (1995). *An unquiet mind: A memoir of moods and madness.* New York: Vintage.

Kaplan, W. A. & Lee, B. A. (1995). *The law of higher education: A comprehensive guide to legal implications of administrative decision making (3rd ed.).* San Francisco, CA: Jossey-Bass.

Jenkins. J. H. (2010). *Pharmaceutical self: The global shaping of experience in an age of psychopharmacology.* Santa Fe, NM: Schools for Advance Research Press.

Karp, D. A. (1996). *Speaking of sadness: Depression, disconnection, and the meaning of illness.* New York: Oxford.

Kesey, K. (1962). *One flew over the cuckoo's nest.* New York: Penguin.

Lin, L., Nigrinis, A. Christidis, P. & Stamm, K. (2015). Psychology workforce: Findings from the American Community Survey. Washington, D. C.: Center for Workforce Studies, American Psychology Association.

*Larson v. Snow College*, 189 F Supp. 2d 1286 (D. Utah 2000).

Liebert, D. (2003). Access to higher education for the mentally ill: A review of trends, implications, and future possibilities for the Americans with Disability Act and the Rehabilitation Act. *The International Journal of Psychosocial Rehabilitation, 7*, 89-100.

Link, B. G. & Phelan, J. C. (1999). The labeling theory of mental disorder (II): The consequences of labeling. In A. V. Horwitz& T. L. Scheid (Eds.), *A handbook for the study of mental health: Social contexts, theories, and systems* (pp. 361-376). New York: Cambridge.

Link, B. G., Phelan, J. C., Bresnahan, M. Stueve, A.,& Pescosolido, B. A. (1999). Public concepts of mental illness: Labels, causes, dangerousness, and social distance. *American Journal of Public Health, 89 (9)*, 1328-1333.

*Maczaczyj v. State of New York*, 956 F. Supp. 403 (W.D. New York 1997).

Maslow, A. H. (2013). *A theory of human motivation: Originally published in Psychological Review, 1943*. USA: Merchant Books.

McGovern, J. (1992). *ADA: Self-evaluation*. Washington, D.C.: National Recreational and Park Association Resource Development Division.

Milgram, S. (1963). Behavioral study of obedience. *Journal of Abnormal and Social Psychology, 67*, 371-378.

Milgram, S. (1969). *Obedience to authority: An experimental view*. NY: Harper.

Morena, C., Laje, G., Blanco, C., et al. (2007). National trends in outpatient diagnosis and treatment of bipolar disorders in youth. Archives of *General Psychiatry, 64 (9)*, 1032-1039.

Mowbray, C. T. & Megivern, D. (1999). Higher education and rehabilitation for people with psychiatric disabilities [Electronic Version]. *Journal of Rehabilitation, 4,* 31-38.

Mulvey, E. P. & Fardella, J. (2000, November/December). Are the mentally ill really violent? *Psychology Today, 39,* 51.

National Alliance of Mental Illness. (2015). Mental health conditions. Retrieved from https://www.nami.org/learn-more/mental-health-conditions

National Science Foundation, National Center for Science and Engineering Statistics. (2013). National Survey of College Graduates Public Use microdatra file and codebook. Retrieved from https://setat.nsf.gov/dpwnload/

Nolen-Hoeksema, S. (2014). *Abnormal psychology* (5th ed.). New York: McGraw-Hill Education.

Osheroff v. Chestnut Lodge, Circuit Court for Montgomery County 66024 (1980).

Pirkis, J., Blood, R. W. Francis, C. & McCallum, K. (2006). On-screen portrayals of mental illness: Extend, nature, and impacts. *Journal of Health Communications, 11,* 523-541. DOI: 10.1080/10810730600755889.

Porter, R. (2002). *Madness: A brief history.* New York: Oxford University Press.

The Brown University Child & Adolescent Psychopharmacology Update. (2014). Moving forward on treating DMDD: Stimulants, parent training, and CBT. Author.

Thomas, V. N., Wilson-Barnett, J. & Goodhart, F. (1998). The role of cognitive-behavioral therapy in the management of pain in patients with sickle cell disease. *Journal of Advanced Nursing, 27 (5),* 1002-1009.

Reske, H. J. (1995, May). Bar applicant wins ADA suit. *American Bar Journal,* 24.*Southeastern Community College v. Davis,* 442 U.S. 397 (19

Sendak, M. (1963). *Where the wild things are.* New York: Harper Collins.

Smail, D. (2005). *Power, interest and psychology: Elements of a social materialist understanding of distress.* United Kingdom: PCCS Books.

Spliter, K. L. (2007). Bipolar disorder diagnosis increases in children and adolescents. *Neuropsychiatry, 8 (10),* 1-23.

Steadman, H. j., Osher, F. C., Robbins, P.c., Case, B. & Samuels, S. (2009). Prevalence of serious mental illness among jail inmates. *Psychiatric Times, 60 (6),* 761-765.

Stefan, S. (2001). *Unequal rights: Discrimination against people with mental disabilities and the Americans with Disabilities Act.* Washington, D.C.: American Psychological Association.

Stringer, H. (2016). Got debt? *Monitor on Psychology, 47 (4),* 52-56.

Styron, W. (1990). *Darkness visible: A memoir of madness.* New York: Oxford Press.

Substance Abuse and Mental Health Services Administration. (2015). National survey on drug use and health. Rockville, MD: author.

Szasz, T. S. (1970). *The manufacture of madness: A comparative study of the inquisition and the mental health movement.* New York: Harper Row.

Szasz, T. S. (1974). *The myth of mental illness: Foundations of a theory of personal conduct.* New York: Harper and Roe.

Taylor, P. J. & Monahan, J. (1996). Commentary: Dangerous patients or dangerous diseases? *British Medical Journal, 312 (2),* 967-969.

U.S. Department of Health and Human Services. (1999). *Mental health: A report of the Surgeon General.* Rockville, MD: U.S. Department of Health and Human Services. Substance Abuse and Mental Health Services Administration, Center for Mental Health Services, National Institutes of Health, National Institute of Mental Health.

United States Department of Education. (2001). *The Americans with Disability Act.* Retrieved September 20, 2002. Retrieved from http://www.ed.gov /offices/OCR/regs/28cfr35.html

United States Department of Education. (2001). *The Rehabilitation Act of 1973*. Retrieved September 20, 2002. Retrieved from http://www.ed.gov/offices/OCR/regs/34cfr104.html

Weber, M. (1949). *The methodology of social science*, (trans. & ed., Edward H. Shils and Henry A. Finch). New York: Free Press.

Wedding, D. & Niemiec, R. M. (2014). *Movies and mental illness: Using films to understand psychopathology*. Boston: Hogrefe.

Winerman, L. (2016). The debt trap. *The Monitor on Psychology*, 47 (4), 44-46.

# Index

personal distress, 19, 35
Ph.D., 115
Pinel, P., 2
premenstrual dysphoric disorder, 54
prevalence, 20, 29, 39, 46, 54
Psy.D., 115
psychache, 10, 36
psychiatrist, 14
psychogenic, 36
psychogenic pain, 36
psycholiterature, 95
psychopharmacology, 15, 27
psychosis, 25, 40, 59, 61, 64, 78, 94, 108, 114
Rush, B., 1
Satcher, D., 32
schizophrenia, 13, 15

selective serotonin reuptake inhibitor, 72
self-actualization, 29
sexual masochism disorder, 35
Shneidman, E., 36
sick role, 48
social cuing, 16
statistically rare, 18
stigma, 51
substance/medication-induced psychotic disorder, 64
suicide contract, 61
Szasz, T., 29, 44
The Rehabilitation Act, 76
transduction, 34
trepanning, 1
vivisect, 107
Watson, J. B., 25
Webber, M., 54

Made in the USA
Columbia, SC
15 January 2021